Jump
From eBay & Etsy To Your Own Money Making Website

By: Karen Lee Fielden

Dedicated to those who, by hook or crook, find
themselves immersed in the world of selling
online and ecommerce.

Karen Lee Fielden
AUTHOR

*Special Thanks and Gratitude to my loving husband
who always supports and believes in me!*

And

My Customers: Past, Present and Future

Contents

INTRODUCTION

Congratulations! You have decided to explore expanding your entrepreneurial activities. You may be operating a business on Etsy, eBay or a similar site. Perhaps you have sold on Amazon. Regardless, you have been running a business, just under someone else's rules.

If you are like many eBay and Etsy sellers, you have often flirted with the idea of creating your own website to sell your wares. You may have tried it once and given up. You may have only entertained the thought and been hesitant out of fear. These worries usually revolve around the following issues:

- I don't have enough time
- What if I do not have customers?
- I am not sure how to go about it
- Can I afford it?
- Who will come to my site?

Sales are shrinking for some sellers on these third party sites. Some are disappointed and angry at the changes that are continually implemented which affect their business. Indeed, we have watched Etsy grow from a small company to a public player on the New York Stock Exchange. We have experienced eBay's ups and downs in the market including a big slap from Google search results and security breaches. Some sellers have experienced a surge or steadiness in sales and have put off creating their own website, believing "if it is not broke, don't fix it".

Yet to rely only on a venue created by others is limiting in several respects. First, if and when there are security breaches on any of these sites, it is highly publicized and this turns many current and prospective buyers to look elsewhere. Second, I have spoke with many people over the years that say, "I don't shop on eBay" or substitute any third party company you like in those quotes. This really limits who your products are exposed to. Third, you are competing with other sellers on the sites. You constantly wonder if enough prospective buyers are seeing your products on these large sites. Current search requirements and listing visibility on Etsy or eBay have many sellers saying "Enough!" They have made the jump and you can too!

My purpose in writing this book is to assist anyone who has entertained this idea but needs a push and help. Don't worry. You can stay on eBay or Etsy if you want. Once you bravely jump in and become a full ecommerce entrepreneur, you will find that there were many resources there to help catch you as you made this leap.

I have written this book for the person who desires a step by step process of creating their own successful site. You can be up and running in a short time. At the end of most chapters, there is a small list of items to accomplish to push you on your quest up the Ecommerce Mountain. What may seem overwhelming to you in the beginning is really quite easy once you know what steps to take.

You will learn how to effectively use methods to get customers to your site. If you have a product that people desire and you follow the formulas provided, you will have sales!

Whether you sell used items or new, digital downloads, hand-made or crafted goods, you can build a beautiful site easily and very cost effectively.

I currently have two websites and I am contemplating a third. I also still sell on eBay and Etsy, at least for now. I will explain to you why I do so a little later in this book.

Most importantly, I will teach you how to find the customers that want your products so that they are coming to your site. Anyone can build a website, but making it profitable is key!

You will find a list of desirable features in deciding upon an ecommerce host along with a glossary of acronyms and terms in the back of this book.

I wish you much success as you branch out, expand your business, and stop putting all your eggs in someone else's basket. You can do this … so let's get started.

When you are successful at getting orders from your own site, I want to hear about it. Please send me a message on your experiences or questions! Contact me at Karen@karenfielden.com

HOW YOU WILL BENEFIT

I created my first ecommerce website in 2010. I had a huge learning curve to navigate. Lucky you! My mistakes are your gain. That site still exists today but it has undergone many changes to be more profitable.

In 2012, I began a second ecommerce site, this time with 2 years of knowledge. It took off 10 times faster than the first one because I knew what to do and I had created a better niche. I want to share that knowledge with you so that you will have a better success rate.

My main impetus for having my own website was to save money on final value fees and to have more control over my business. Rules and requirements change so often, especially on eBay. It became burdensome to keep up with and aggravating to be treated as a constant beginner despite the fact that I was a long term successful seller on their site.

Yes, it was and is their site … not mine or yours. You may be allowed to have a store or many free listings, rated top seller, etc., but it is their site and overall brand. All third party sites can kick you off without much notice. They can limit and restrict how much you can sell or what categories. They can push other seller's products ahead of yours in the search game. They allow affiliate marketers the ability to advertise the same products you are selling.

You have your own reasons for wanting your own money making site and there are so many benefits that it does not make sense to waste time in just thinking about it. You will enjoy:

- Branding and building your own business
- Building customers loyal to your business
- No final value fees
- Easily accept a multitude of payment options
- No longer a victim of unfair feedback

- Not wasting time on phone with customer service over customer disputes.
- Have total control of your policies – you make the rules
- Not subjected to the uncertain future of a platform site
- Your listings are the only ones on your site.
- Competing products from other sellers are not advertised on your site
- You decide your return policies and terms

Recently, I read on a forum about a distraught Etsy seller who had her shop closed down abruptly by the company. She said this was some huge misunderstanding, stating that she had written a fellow seller on the Etsy platform with a question about her product. Somewhere within the communication, Etsy's system flagged it as an attempt to do an "offline" deal and shut her down immediately. She stated that Etsy agreed, after looking at the communication, that she was not in violation and would be reinstated in a day. A week later, nothing had been resolved. Her Etsy store was still restricted and she could not get anyone to respond or work with her. I asked if she had her own website. Unfortunately, she did not.

There are so many situations that can arise when you have little control. This story is typical of many sellers who have suddenly found themselves in a horrible predicament. The most difficult time to create your own site is in an emergency situation.

Creating your own site and learning to find your customers is not something that is so difficult, but it is work. The work is mental, not physical. It is creative and satisfying. You will feel and be accomplished.

Do not let fear keep you from this opportunity. There is nothing to fear at all. You will have wild successes and wild failures along the way and you will learn from each. As you hone your skills at being an ecommerce merchant, you will enjoy flexibility and freedom coupled with hard work that most people are too timid to try.

What Flavor Is Your Future Website?

Consumers are often overwhelmed if you have too many categories and product choices. Many sites make it difficult to navigate with so many different things to choose from. Online stores are now focusing on more specific product lines to attract their customer base. One of my early mistakes was trying to be everything and offer too much selection.

The flavor of your ecommerce site should be sharp and tangy. The texture should be crisp, not blended and mushy. People need to know immediately when they land there what you sell. If they feel overwhelmed by the wide variety of inventory, they tend to click off the site. This is accomplished by having a niche.

The products you sell should be displayed in a natural, logical flow on either the main page of the site or in the categories that appear on the home page if you are using a cleaner look. Carrying more precisely chosen inventory is another advantage of offering the products your customers really want. Your business can run leaner with more predictable profit margins. Obtaining inventory will be easier and you will move it faster for the right amount of money.

I have lived through having all my profits tied up in inventory. These were items I purchased at the height of the selling season that were really not my current hot sellers. I did this with the belief in mind that if I had "more" items, I would have more sales.

At the end of one month, I had sold over twenty thousand dollars worth of merchandise and had hardly any money to show for it. I thought my money was disappearing out of my bank account. I must have more money than this! Careful analysis showed that I had too much inventory left of at the end of the month. This truly diminishes your net profits from your business endeavors. Each time I looked at the wall of inventory in my office I would say to myself: "there's your money".

Sticking with items you know sell consistently and not branching out too much in the beginning is advisable. For some reason, I just thought I had to build some huge site where I had so much stuff that anyone who landed there would buy something. This did not happen. In fact, many shoppers may have felt confused by too many choices. The site was beautiful, but did not come together in a cohesive way.

Selection is good, but I have seen sites make it with only one product. If it is something people want, they come to purchase that one item. Most ecommerce sites are going to offer a selection of items and most consumers do want that. However, too much choice can just lead to complete confusion on the site.

Imagine walking into any store and immediately noticing that it is not organized well and the products are not displayed in a manner that attracts your eye. This is what happened with my first internet attempt. I did get orders but had no money to show for it because I junked up my store.

Unfortunately, I had no guide book or mentor and made another mistake. With stubborn determination, I decided that my products hanging on the wall would sell for retail. I was not going to discount them. Some of them did sell at retail, but it took a long time. I eventually heavily discounted most of them to move them out.

Now, as I go into each season, I know what sells and I order that. I may test market an extremely small quantity of another product that I believe to be promising, but only <u>if it fits into my niche</u>. Provided that product sells, I order more in accordance with the current buying trend. I deal with manufacturers who can supply me quickly. I sold far less products last year, but made more profit using this technique. This also means there was less time spent packing orders.

Although I am adept at shopping online and I have purchased from Amazon frequently, I find their site contains too many items. Visually, the site is not appealing to me. I will also purchase the same items from another website, especially if the price is comparable or I will receive free shipping. Somehow, it feels more personal.

If you have stayed in one particular area on eBay or Etsy and sell only new clothing, vintage clothing, auto parts, craft materials, handmade items, you will find it easy to create your niche website. However, if you have used retail arbitrage to sell a multitude of different items, you will need to determine what products you can have on your new site that will work for you. Many current and former eBay sellers may have sold such a vast array of items that it is hard to narrow down what that niche will be. I recommend looking again at what sells well and gives you a good profit margin.

In the next chapter, we will look at those who have gone before you and how they have created their niche. Several of these entrepreneurs began on eBay.

Ninja Tip: Be your own little guru market niche

ACTION LIST

1. Grab a notebook or binder and realize that this book you are reading is interactive to a degree like a workbook. You will be identifying factors that only relate to your business and the use of notes during this reading will help you.
2. Look at your products and determine who the buying audience is for those items. This is important because we want to know where those people hang out on the internet for marketing purposes later. What are their approximate ages, gender, and interests? What countries do they live in?
3. Do you have products that always sell? Make a list of those products and include your profit margins on each.

Their Stories

In accordance with your action list in the previous chapter, determine what products are selling and who is your buying audience? Keep that in mind as you read this chapter so we can really apply this to your business. We will look at the brief stories of some who have gone before you with their own niche sites. Looking at what others have done successfully assists us greatly in where we want to head ourselves. Plus, it is always fun and informative to see what other businesspeople are doing.

I have no affiliation with these sites. Take the time to visit them and click around each one or perform searches for similar sites on your own.

- Make notes of what you like and what does not appeal to you.
- When you land on the site, can you tell what they sell very quickly?
- Is the site easy to navigate?
- Is it easy to find particular items?
- Do you like what the company is projecting on their "About Us" page?
- What is their return policy?
- What is the quality of the product photos?
- What do they name their products?
- Do they have good product descriptions?

These are all considerations to take into account when you are designing your site. By looking at others, we can find the faults with them and know that is something we want to avoid. We can also find what they are doing right and use that information to help ourselves.

Vintage Apparel & Accessories Category

I performed a search for used and vintage clothing. I found www.rustyzipper.com which specializes in vintage clothing for all ages including Hawaiian shirts, bell bottoms, disco shirts, and more. They claim to be the first online vintage clothing store and have had this internet presence for twenty years. Impressive!

Rusty Zipper sells clothing for men, women, and children, along with accessories and sewing patterns that are also vintage. It appears they are a big and broad site, but very specialized.

Blend of Used and New Apparel:

Another very successful, yet more recent used clothing site is Nasty Gal (www.nastygal.com). Sophie Amoruso, the founder of Nasty Gal was kicked off eBay in 2008 and immediately started working frantically to create a website with the customer base she had established from eBay.

When we look at the Nasty Gal site, we can quickly determine her niche. First she appears to carry only clothing for women. She does not handle clothing for men or children. She breaks her products down on her site into new or vintage. I see that she has recently added a new category: Gifts + Home.

As soon as you land on the website, you know it is about clothing for women. The models are very edgy looking, a word that Sophie highly dislikes but is broad enough to describe the look.

Nevertheless, this lady took a small business on eBay selling used clothing and now owns a multi-million dollar company based in California with a fulfillment warehouse in Kentucky. The company is now designing new clothing collections with the Nasty Gal label as well. Sophie has a New York Times bestselling book about her business chronicles called #GirlBoss. Prior to her online sales, she worked menial jobs and has no college education.

Used Golf Equipment

Golf Avenue is a Canadian company that began selling used golf equipment on eBay. They now sell thousands of used golf items monthly on their site www.golfavenue.ca

Utilizing used golf equipment only as their niche, the men behind this company which started up in 2006 show a true vision of their business ideals and products on their site. This business began accidently. The founders saw $150.00 golf clubs marked down to $50 in a golf equipment store. They immediately knew they could turn those for a good profit on eBay. It turned out the golf store was buying back a customer's old golf clubs when they sold them new ones. This set the entire business into motion for the guys. As fees increased on eBay, the two set out to sink a hole in one on their own website.

Jewelry

There is so much jewelry available worldwide in brick and mortar stores and online. If you sell jewelry, how will you create a niche for yourself in this crowded market?

I came across www.larimarket.com doing a search for jewelry from the Caribbean. They carry all aspects of jewelry such as pendants, necklaces, bracelets and more, all with larimar stones. I like their About Us page.

Larimarket has a niche. The probably have quite a few repeat customers. I noticed they use a very clean black and white scheme to their website, allowing the beautiful jewelry to be the stand-out star.

One of the items I like on their site is "15 Reasons To Shop At Larimarket". However, the text is very small. I think larger bulleted points may stand out better as this turns into a lot of reading.

Looking for another niche within jewelry, I found Michelle's Vintage Jewelry (www.michellesvintagejewelry.com). Many of these items are on eBay and Etsy, yet she has her own site and since she has a "sold" link at the bottom of the home page, we can see that these antique pieces are selling. I say this because I know some of you sell used and vintage jewelry and I want you to know this is totally possible to do with your own site.

The site is simple and well categorized. I thought the user experience could benefit from photos that can be shown in an enlarged view. Since each product is unique, customer reviews would be useless. To compensate, she has created a page with customer raves and reviews.

On Michelle's About Us page, she includes awards received, books used for researching her niche, and more.

She has a blog which is great. Her last post was in 2014, however. Her Facebook page could use more frequent posts and "likes".

Used Video Games

In 1999, Hendricks, a college student bought a used Sega Genesis console and 10 games which he sold on eBay for profit. He continued to sell used games for the next four years while attending school. Now in 2015, www.jjgames.com is going strong and has grown into a more than full time business with 12 employees and a warehouse. Specializing only in used and vintage video equipment and games, they are further proof that having a niche and working it is the way to go.

Antique Electronics

You will find replacement parts for a Leslie Keyboard, tubes for amplifiers and more at www.tubesandmore.com. While their "About Us" page did not tell any history of their company, they are a definite niche business.

Vintage Kitchen

Closing their eBay store in 2007, Classic Kitchens and More appears to have a great site with lots of things people want for their kitchen that have timeless quality. Selling almost all vintage American made cooking and dinnerware, I see a great selection and thriving business. www.classickitchensandmore.com

Health & Beauty

I recently ordered two items from **Pure Formulas** who resells health and beauty products. They shipped immediately and free. When I opened the well packed box, they included my invoice and a couple of cards advertising two other products. It all looked very professional. On top of this paperwork and the first thing you saw as you opened it was a unique marketing piece printed on slick card stock that said "This order could be FREE! Find out how". On the back of the two sided piece it showcased small photos of customers with their products. It invited you to post a photo of you with your products and five lucky winners would receive their next order free. You could post to the company's page on Instagram, Facebook or Twitter. Make sure you check out their "About Us" page on their site. It was one of the best I have seen.

I will reorder from them. The products are consumable items I go through about every 45 days. I was not satisfied with the last place I purchased them, especially the packaging. They did not put any shipping tape on the oddly shaped box and my products were nearly falling out when it arrived. There was no invoice or thank you from the previous company. Do you know who the previous company was? Should I say? Well, let's just say that they dominate the industry and have many warehouses. It also took a week to arrive to me from their warehouse that is two hours from my house.

Pure Formulas gave great service, free priority shipping, professional packaging and smart marketing. This is a small business that I like supporting. See: www.pureformulas.com

By taking a few moments to look at these sites, you get a good idea of what you could do with your own. As you view the sites, jot down in a notebook what features you like and dislike.

ACTION LIST

1. Visit other successful sites and look at what is working for them and also what you do not like
2. Just for fun, write an "About Us" page for your future site. It could just be one sentence, a paragraph or several. Just put down your initial thoughts. Save your notes to refer back to as you create your own "About Us" page very soon.

NOTES:

Your Niche

Chances are you have already found your niche of items to sell. You've spent time learning the market and know your profit margins. I believe if you are selling items you personally value, you will be more engaged and successful because of it.

If you are a seller crafting art or hand-made items, obviously you have a love for your products. It's time to showcase them properly on your own site!

If you have previously sold a wide variety of items on eBay, you may need to think about what products you have to offer and who the buying customers are. For instance, if you have thus far sold a combination of pre-owned clothing, video games, toys and DVD's, you may want to narrow things for your online store.

Begin by determining which items have brought in the most net revenue and consistently sell. Which items seem to sit longer and are harder to move? Which items are more competitive to sell? Answering these questions will point you in the right direction and show what demand there is for a particular niche.

Next, determine the mass demand for your products you have now or those you may add later. To analyze trends and how high the demand is for your product, utilize the power of Google Trends (www.google.com/trends). Here you can enter product keywords and see if the item is trending upward or down in popularity over a specific time period.

While looking at the product at Google Trends, check other close companion products or keywords to see if they are trending higher in searches than the particular product you are considering.

Confused? Go to the Google Trends site. In the search box at the top, type in any product you want. Instantly, a chart will pop up that shows searches conducted for that product keyword over time. Also note that it will be more helpful if you type in the singular name of the item instead of plural. If I want to search lava lamps, I will type in lava lamp (without the plural "s"). This will bring up results for lava lamp and lava lamps. But if I type in lava lamps, it will leave out lava lamp because of the plural "s". It's just how computers think!

Let's pretend you are considering selling tea online. There are many types and you will want to compare them side by side. Let's look at green tea versus matcha tea. Although green tea has continuously trended upward each year in searches, the lesser known matcha tea is showing a sudden spike of interest. It still does not show as much search activity as green tea, but if I were selling teas, I would consider selling both. We do not know how long matcha tea will trend upward and green tea has shown a consistent interest by tea drinkers. So, that may lead me to believe that I should stock more green tea, but definitely have some of the matcha as well.

Google Trends is easy to use and you can do side by side comparisons of keywords or actual products.

Step By Step:
Go to: https://www.google.com/trends/
On the right hand side, choose the main country you are selling within for this search. In the search bar, type in the product name
A graph will appear with interest levels by year.

If you move your mouse over the peaks and valleys of the item, you will see actual numbers. You may also check the boxes next to this chart to show you recent news about the item and the forecasted level of interest for the future.

If you scroll down, you will see a world map with areas of the world highlighted to show interest in this item by country.

If you would like to do a side-by-side comparison of another product with this one, click on "add term" near the top of the page. Type in the new product and you will notice that it will be highlighted with a different color.

You may now compare the interest levels side-by-side. You may add even more products to compare side by side with each having a different color on the graph.

If you add the word organic to green tea and matcha tea, notice you get different numbers and interest levels. This hints that by changing one element or condition of the products you are considering, you could put many more dollars into your pocket!

The chart below shows a search I did on four terms:

Scented Candles – Potpourri - Scented Wax – Scentsy

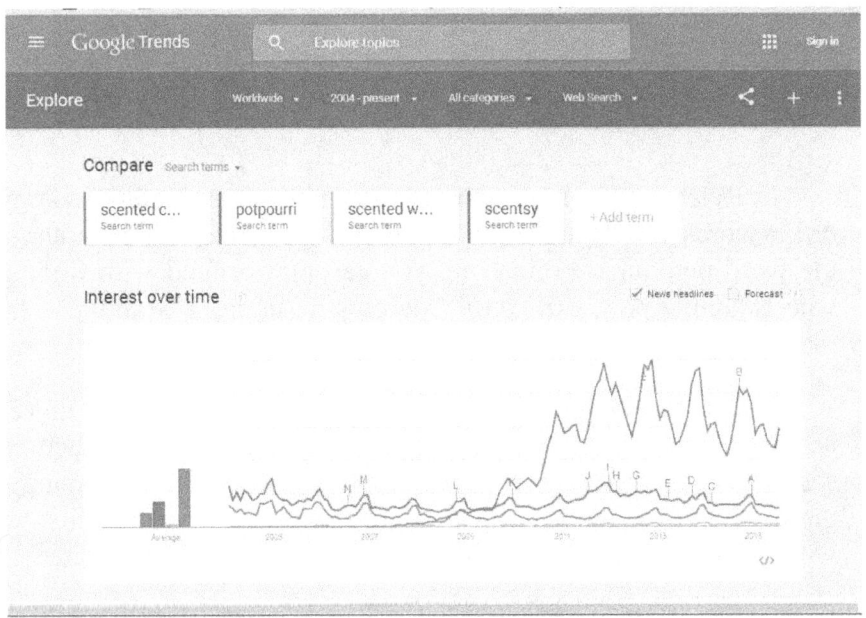

We see that Scentsy (represented in green if you are seeing this in color) is much higher in searches than all of the others. In case you are not familiar, Scentsy is a brand name scented wax company. I believe they may be sold only through independent consultants or distributors. I would take that into account when looking at this because many of the searches may have been people looking for a money making opportunity that "smells good".

I was surprised to see that a search for potpourri (red) had higher search results than scented wax or scented candles, ranking in at second most popular keyword. That would make me investigate further to see what people are searching for related to potpourri. You can find that out easily by navigating down on the page to see the following.

Related searches

scented candles potpourri scented wax scentsy

Topics	Top	Rising	Queries	Top	Rising
Potpourri	100		the potpourri	100	
			make potpourri	95	
			potpourri pot	80	
			herbal potpourri	75	
			potpourri incense	75	
			potpourri smoke	50	
			potpourri catalog	50	

Related Searches is an area that shows us the terminology or keywords people are using by percentage levels when searching the word potpourri. From here, you can play around with finding who is selling potpourri, profit margins on it, etc. I would also do more testing for demand in the marketplace.

A third element to consider when choosing products to sell is: are you connected to these products or passionate about them in some way? Are you knowledgeable about the products? Having a thorough knowledge of your products and what their benefits are will assist you with content marketing which we will cover later.

Many of you already have a great niche that is working well for you on eBay or Etsy. Your need for research may not be something you need to spend a lot of time on. These tools are handy to have, however, should you want to expand into another product line and/or separate niche website.

For those who look at your current products and wonder how to make that into a niche, pay special attention to the examples of those who have gone before you onto their own websites. Use Google Trends and other tools to do your market research.

If you sell pre-owned clothing, what brands are people looking for the most in jeans, shirts, shorts, shoes, etc. Do certain sizes sell better that may be harder to find like big and tall for men or petite, maternity or plus sizes for women?

I hope that you already know your niche and can now begin immediately on your website creation. If you are still determining that, take your time as it is one of the critical elements to your success. I want to repeat that: having products to sell that people want is absolutely the number one factor in whether or not you will make money. The time you spend researching this will pay off for you.

If I were to begin a third website, I would spend the majority of my time finding the right niche and then determining if I could make a profit off those products.

ACTION LIST

1. Thoroughly research your niche or ideas you have for a niche using Google Trends. If you believe sufficient demand is there for the products, look at profit margins that you can realistically achieve in a competitive environment.
2. As you research, jot down keywords associated with the products you sell. You may need these keywords later to put into meta tag descriptions for your new site. This will help you place higher in search results. Those search terms can also give you ideas for how you will find your customers and market to them as well.

Providers – A Close Look

When I first began an ecommerce site for one of my businesses, I chose one of the less expensive ecommerce hosts that I could customize to my liking. It was only $15 per month. I had orders and traffic despite the fact that I had not begun any advertising. I was delighted that these were new customers, not anyone I had dealt with prior from eBay or Etsy.

As time went on, I kept noticing how limited I was with the site and how it really did not have the professional look that I wanted, nor certain features such as abandoned shopping cart. This feature notifies you when a shopper has placed items in the cart and not paid for them. You can then decide if you want to send an incentive to them such as free shipping or a discount coupon code. You may automate this process.

After shopping many features and rates of the different ecommerce hosts, I chose Bigcommerce to host the site. I paid for the premium plan and assistance to migrate all of my product listings to the new site and to create 301 redirects or backlinks so that I did not lose the search engine placements that had already been established.

At the sales rep's encouragement, I also made the mistake of attempting to move the site to Bigcommerce right in the middle of my busiest time of year. What is wrong with me? It did not work out. I had poor response time from their tech support. My sales ended up suffering for the season, and I did not like the way that variations such as sizes and colors were set up for selection on their platform.

I went through a lot of self-induced stress during this very busy 4th quarter of the year. Once it was over, I chose a third site. This time I had more time to put into overseeing the transfer and did the majority of the site creation on my own to make sure it was accurate. No one cares about your site and business like you do, even when you are paying others good money to do so. Another lesson learned.

Choose a web host provider that is dependable and you can grow with as your business grows. Take advantage of those free trial days they give you and really find out if you like how it feels to set the site up and enter in quite a few product listings. If you sell items that have selections such as color or size, pay special attention to how easy or difficult it is to include that in each product listing.

Now that I have tried so many, I will detail each one in the following pages that I believe to be the best considerations for an ecommerce start-up that has little to mid-level technical experience.

I have not received any monetary consideration for mentioning these sites whatsoever. I have either used their trial periods or actually used them as my choice of an ecommerce host. I may in the future receive affiliate fees from one or more of these hosts on my author website or blog. As of this writing, I do not receive any consideration.

3DCart

3dCart is easy to use to set up your site. A wizard is included to walk you through the process. Additionally, there are videos you can watch that show you exactly what to click on to accomplish a particular task. You may also enter a design mode on your site that allows for "drag and drop" creation or editing.

There are over 80 free templates to choose from that are very professional looking. All of these included layouts for mobile phones and tablets. There were themes ranging from fashion clothing, eyewear, electronics, wine, food, cosmetics, services, and more.

You may also pay for a premium template, if desired. The option is available to have your entire website look customized at a much higher cost. This is true at all of the companies profiled here.

Please keep in mind when shopping for a template or theme for your site that you will be able to change the pictures – logos – categories – hyperlinks to click on also such as Blog – About Us, etc. This is true on all of the shopping software hosting sites I will be reviewing.

Keep any welcome emails when you sign up for a site and do not delete. Sometimes, they contain special links you will need in the future.

3dcart has gift registry and reward points, along with other promotions such as B1G1 Free – Free Shipping – Bulk Discounts. On the professional plan, it even includes "make an offer" option.

A Facebook store is built into 3dcart, along with your mobile store version and a blog. They have 24x7 tech support – very important at times.

Currently, new users are given free adwords credit ranging from $175 - $225.00 and a "personal guru" session from their staff.

All of the features with 3dcart are really great except I did not care for the fact that they have maximums on the number of visits per month to your website i.e., bandwidth. In addition, you are limited to the number of products you can have listed unless you go with the higher priced plan. Depending upon what you sell, this may not matter to you. Do check them out at www.3dcart.com

BigCommerce

This is a great company. My issues I had with them were me going against my good judgment and timing. Big Commerce is also favored by many of my ecommerce friends.

Their middle plan is currently $79.95, a little pricey if you are just venturing into ecommerce on your own as a small seller. If you are a large seller, this plan would work for you and I would recommend taking a look at it.

I was disappointed with the technical support. I paid for the most expensive plan and felt that waiting on hold for 45 minutes or more to speak with technical support was just too long. Perhaps they have corrected this situation.

Big Commerce has a ton of bells and whistles for their ecommerce customers including the abandoned cart check-out, multi-channel tools for eBay, social networking tools and more.

It is easy to edit the look of your site with their Style Editor which allows you to choose header background colors, drop down menus and footer area.

BigCommerce claims that their clients have "Google domination" in search results due to the way their platform is designed. I cannot say if this is true or not.

The ability to have a Facebook store is included along with social share buttons for all major sharing sites. Email integration is included with at least four email service providers.

They have B2B capabilities. Inventory management can only be achieved on the Bigcommerce platform by adding the third party app by Stitchlabs.

You can begin a 15 day trial without submitting payment information up front. Please note that BigCommerce charges a 1.5% transaction fee on all sales if you are on the lowest plan (Standard). While not huge, this is something we are trying to get away from, right?

Miva

Miva Merchant is a long time supplier of website hosting with cart checkout. Miva can handle smaller boutique size websites and much larger sites like TaylorSwift.com.

Some persons report ease of use and others say there may be more of a learning curve here for a beginner. If you are fairly experienced, I would give Miva a serious look as the platform is designed to grow with your business no matter how large it becomes.

Miva has the ability to integrate with eBay and Amazon. Their boutique plan currently is less than $50 per month. They have 24x7 US based telephone support.

Your ecommerce site is search engine friendly in design from the beginning and you can enter an unlimited amount of products.

Like 3Dcart, they do not offer unlimited bandwidth, but do have generous amounts for each plan.

If you want your website to also have a wholesale portal log-in for other businesses who purchase wholesale from you, Miva allows for that in their B2B feature.

Please note that after your first year with Miva, your credit card will be charged yearly instead of monthly for your fees. This could make a difference with some sellers. There is a 30 day trial period. You are charged in advance for that trial and refunded if not satisfied. Check them out at www.miva.com

Shopify

One of the best features they have is the ability to create buy buttons on Pinterest. Additionally, you can integrate your store directly into your company's Facebook page. Shopify is also now introducing buy buttons for Twitter.

I have found it easy to use and set up a site. A wizard is included to walk you through the process. Additionally, there are videos that show you exactly what to click on to accomplish a particular task. You may also enter a design mode on your site that allows for "drag and drop" creation or editing.

There are many free templates to choose from, but not as many as 3dcart has. I did like the layout of some of their fashion templates much better than 3dcart. The templates include layouts for mobile phones and tablets. You may also pay for a premium template, if desired. The option is available to have your entire website look customized at a much higher cost.

Shopify has an abandoned cart feature on some of the plans just like Bigcommerce. You will also have the ability to sell gift certificates plus receive 24x7 tech support – very important at times.

You can begin with a website for less than $30 a month and no set up fees. If you have less than 25 products, they have a starter plan for $14 per month with less features but unlimited bandwidth or visits per month.

They have payment options for their credit card processor without you needing a payment gateway. You may also use this same processing service to do POS (Point of Sale) transactions. This could be really handy if you have a brick and mortar store or you set up at art fairs or flea markets on weekends. You simply use the Shopify app on your tablet or smart phone to process payments.

Shopify also integrates with Paypal, Stripe, First Data, and many others including the ability to process Bitcoin. Check them out at www.shopify.com

Volusion

This company has been successfully helping online merchants for awhile now. For an online seller, you can begin for as low as $9 per month but you will only have online support instead of being able to pick up the phone and call.

Volusion's plan at $35 per month (up to 1000 products) looks much better for what anyone starting out will need. If you plan on continuing to sell on Amazon or EBay, they have a plan at $75 per month (up to 10,000 products) that integrates with those sites so that you are not entering your listings twice or three times. Bandwidth (number of visits) per month is limited on all plans except the premium. Volusion offers a free trial at www.volusion.com

30

E-Commerce Host Comparison

	3DCart	BigCommerce	MIVA	Shopify	Volusion
Abandon Cart		★		★	★
Email Integration	★	★		★	★
24x7 Phone Support	★	★	★	★	★
Unlimited Bandwidth		★		★	
Shipping Integration		★	★	★	
Responsive Design		★	★	★	★
Google Analytics Module	★	★	★	★	★
Unlimited Products		★	★	★	
Gift Certificates		★		★	★
Facebook Store	★	★		★	★
Blog	★	★		★	
Buy x Get y Feature	★	★	★		★
Wish List	★	★			★
Store Coupons	★	★	★	★	★
Inventory Tracking			★	★	★
Pinterest Buy Buttons				★	
Twitter Buy Buttons				★	
Ebay Integration		★	★	★	★
Amazon Integration		★	★	★	★
B2B and/or B2C		★	★	★	★
Reporting/Analytics		★	★	★	
Product Reviews		★		★	★
3rd Party App Live Chat	★	★		★	★
Multiple Language		★		★	
Smart Phone Managable				★	★

Create infographics   infogr.am

All of these companies have pros and cons. Nothing is just perfect but do not let that stop you! For the majority of first-timers, all of the suggestions mentioned above will work for your new store. There are hosts for less money, but they are often missing the features you are going to need to be successful. Indeed, I tried some of those website hosting companies when I began. Remember, I mentioned you will gain from my mistakes!

Utilize the trials on any hosts that you are considering. Once you are in and trying their software out, pay special attention to what it takes to enter your listings and upload photos. Go through all the motions of setting up several different products as a test. This is especially critical if you sell items with variations such as sizes, colors, etc. From testing each platform out, you can get an idea of how easy or difficult it will be to manage your products on the site and input listings.

At first, it will be slow inputting products into the site. This is normal. You will gain speed with repetition and familiarity. For this reason, enter several products into the site during your trial run. However, I have always found entering listings on my own websites much faster than eBay, maybe slower than Etsy.

Do not be afraid to use "copy and paste" from your listing descriptions on eBay or Etsy into your new trial site. If time is one of the things that kept you from building your own site, we want that to not remain a barrier. Time is always critical for any business person. However, do go back and revise those product descriptions before your site goes "live". The reason you want to do this is search engines are picking up these descriptions across the internet. If they pick up your description on eBay and your same description on your site, this may or may not work in your favor, depending upon what you are selling. It could push your website into a situation where it will receive fewer visitors on those products because the search engine sees it as a duplicate. Fresh product descriptions or even just changing the sentences around will help you in search.

When choosing which site to use, determine whether it has the ability to import your listings from eBay or Etsy. Many do including Miva and Shopify. Test this feature out and see how well it works. This can be a real time saver.

Make sure the website host has a template you like that can be easily modified with your company logo, photos you select, categories and such. Check to see if you can easily change the colors of certain items on the home page.

Also note that many people like using Wordpress in conjunction with a shopping cart like Woo-Commerce. If you are tech savvy, go ahead and consider using this as your platform. You can get Godaddy to host the site and use Wordpress to form your site. You will need add-ons for ecommerce such as Woo-Commerce to take payments and provide a checkout feature. There are quite a few ecommerce stores built on this platform and those users seem to very much like it. This book, however, is aimed at people who are looking for more of a plug and play system when it comes to their new website and that is the only reason I did not feature Wordpress as an option, as it is not really a single packaged product, but something you put together.

ACTION LIST

1. Choose at least 2 different companies to experience a trial run with.
2. During your trials, give special consideration to how easy it is for you to use the site, get information when you need it, enter product listings and upload photos.

NOTES:

Money Flowing From Multiple Sources

As mentioned earlier, I continue to sell on eBay and Etsy. I use both sites as fishing ponds to catch a portion of my new customers. By doing this, I am technically a multi-channel seller.

Selling on multiple sites can be tricky. If you only have one or two of a particular item, you must delete it from the other sites once it has sold on one venue to keep customers from being disappointed. This can be accomplished manually or by using a third-party provider that specializes in inventory management.

Give your best prices on your own website, leaving room for enough profit to offer occasional specials like a percentage off or free shipping. If you plan to continue selling on third party sites like eBay or Etsy, make sure you keep your prices higher on each product to cover your final value fees and other associated costs of selling on their platforms.

One thing that really spurs eBay sellers on is when free listings are offered. The offer will come to your email box and have a selected time period of 2-7 days in which you can list more products with no listing fees. For my business, it can sometimes be a trap! I have found that *money flows where my attention goes*. When I spent my time entering a ton of listings on eBay, I was ignoring my own websites and the marketing I would normally do to drive business. eBay would become overly crowded with all the new listings that sellers were inputting, thus not resulting in many sales for me compared to the time lost on my own sites.

I currently keep the smallest store level on eBay. When additional free listings are offered, I have a file of about 200 additional listings that I can upload very quickly and be done with it. This allows me to put my time and focus on where I really want to grow: my own branded websites.

ACTION LIST:

1. Decide if you will continue selling on third party sites. If so, determine whether you will need assistance with inventory management because this would be the time to look at web hosts that may have apps that can integrate that for you between the sites.
2. Make sure your product prices on your website are more attractive
3. If you are an eBay seller, consider making a folder with listing templates of additional items you can upload during free listings.

Attracting Customers

One of the largest fears preventing people from pursuing their own website is the malingering question: How can I get customers to the site? It is true that almost anyone can create a website. Improving traffic and attracting customers to come, look, and purchase is paramount. Potential customers that are browsing your site are wanted and needed, yet more must be done in order to entice them to click the buy button and become a "conversion". In the following chapters, I will step you through many different avenues of acquiring customers. I will also teach you how to find where your customers hang out.

Chances are you came across this book by an email or a social networking site. You may have seen it on Amazon and purchased it directly. There are thousands of books on Amazon. If I relied on you just accidently discovering this book amidst hundreds or thousands on the site, we may have never crossed paths. It is the same for what you sell. You must utilize many ways to get your products in front of your potential customers.

At the time you create your website or shortly thereafter, I would recommend that you start out with the following free business accounts:

Facebook – Twitter - Pinterest

Instructions are in each chapter for creating the free business accounts.

For coordinated social network marketing, you need to have all of your accounts in your business name with your business logo. I will explain how to navigate and use each one of these sites individually in the upcoming chapters. However, an email program wherein you can send email to your customers you have acquired to date is at the top of the list. We will cover that soon.

ACTION LIST:

    a. Purchase your domain name for your website. There are many different places such as Godaddy to do this. Decide if you want to pay extra to keep the ownership of the domain private.

    b. Create your company logo if you do not already have one. Just search logo creators on the internet

    c. Consider whether you want a company slogan and what that will be. Will it be attached to your logo or separate?

NOTES:

Setting Up Your Website

All of the website hosts I have recommended have easy to use navigation. Each will be different in its ease of use and the way things are organized. All should have help sections and many video tutorials or wizard assistants to get you up and running.

If this is your first time setting up a website, it can feel frustrating because you are new. Stay the course and look at all the wonderful help features the host provider has available. Most of these providers have very detailed information on how to do just about anything. Many have video instruction step by step. When all else fails, call them and get help over the phone. I said it before and I will say it again: You can do this!

There should be a section on your website you are building that allows you to choose the way your customer can check out (pay) and how much information to capture from them.

When you find this section which is generally under Settings/Checkout, consider allowing the customer to checkout as a guest without officially registering with your site. This is especially helpful for those in a hurry. Otherwise, some customers become frustrated and abandon their shopping cart. However, realize if they do not register, you have no way to retarget the customer with the abandoned shopping cart feature.

I would make sure you require the first and last names, along with their phone number and email address. If there is an option for the Ship To field to default to the same information entered into their home address field, allow it to default there and they can change that, if desired. Again, keeping things simple for the customer will assist in them not abandoning the shopping cart.

Paypal will only allow the customer to ship to their address listed on their account with Paypal. However, credit card processing companies will allow them to ship elsewhere. This is very handy for those shipping gifts.

Decide what your refund policy will be and post it in the section allotted for that on your website. Many sites give you a general policy to go by and you may adjust that and change it to your specific needs. If you need help with this, look at what other ecommerce stores are doing to have a guide.

Many website hosts offer a setting to pause your store. If you are a one woman or man operation and you intend to take a vacation, have a family emergency, etc., this setting will allow your store to still be seen by customers. However, they will not be able to make purchases during that time. You can also post a message on your home page that states something like:

"We appreciate your visit to our store. We are currently closed until September 7th for inventory"

Your conversion rate will increase if you offer a phone number for customers to call. This greatly enhances a buyer's confidence that you are a legitimate site and someone they can contact if needed. In the beginning, I used to pay for a toll-free number. Now, I have a separate free Google phone number for each site. I can control what hours the Google phone will ring; forward to whatever phone I want it to ring to; and speak face to face on Google with a customer if I choose to. You can also set it up to free voicemail so that you never answer it, only return messages left.

This is available at https://www.**google**.com/**voice**

Okay, a customer is on your home page. Now what? Offer a call to action – one may be free shipping for orders over a certain dollar amount. Another call to action item might be a five or ten percent discount for a limited time. By making it only for a limited time, this may convert the browser into a paid customer.

Have you ever visited a website and the first thing they want you to do before you can even view what they have to offer is sign up for their newsletter list or create an account? I quickly click off those sites. This is something you will have to think about as you create your site. Do you want customers to <u>have</u> to sign up or <u>choose</u> to sign up?

I have been buying items online since 1998 and often do the majority of my Christmas shopping from the internet. A shop that requires me to give all of me before I even see what they have to offer never gets my business. I want to look around first.

Registering with your site should be the next step when they want to purchase. You may also choose to have the guest option to shop on your site. Some people are in a hurry, especially if they are shopping from their smart phone. They just need to order an item and they do not want to go through a registration process to do so where they have to create a password. As the online shop owner, you will still receive all their pertinent information such as name, address, and email with their order they placed.

Here is what I do for my sites on whether to make them register or not for purchasing. During my slower seasons, I want them to register. When they do that, I have an abandoned shopping cart to work with. If they just place items in their cart as a guest and the system does not pick up who they are, I have no opportunity to have the system retarget them with an email inviting them to come back and complete the purchase.

During the busy fourth quarter, I may decide to change and allow guest checkout. This tends to be a time of year that people are in a huge hurry and I want it to be simple and fast. As the website owner, it is good to have the option of either one or both.

Product reviews are hot! These little opinionated blurbs give buyers the confidence to go ahead and purchase. It also gives great feedback information critical for customer decision making. One very popular item I sell runs a little tight and feedback from customers has been that the dimensions of the item are right, but it feels snug. As potential buyers read these comments, they can decide whether to order the next size up.

Sites without reviews show less sales or conversion rates. Sites with reviews offer potential customers more knowledge to make a decision. In this information age, people are curious and want to make a purchase online with confidence.

I belong to a group of entrepreneurs who are often asked to look at ecommerce websites and see why they are not selling products. One of the most common problems I see are no product reviews. It is slow going getting reviews in the beginning. Only a very small percentage of customers take the time to leave a review. This reminds me to ask if you are enjoying the information I have put together for you in this book so far? Would you please leave me a review on Amazon or the site you purchased from?

Post sale follow-up is a great way to ask a customer to review the product. Some customers will just do it without being asked, but few. You may want to create a standard email that asks the customer a few days after product delivery to review their purchase. Thank them and let them know you want them to be a repeat customer. You may perhaps offer them 10% off their next order with a coupon code. You might personalize the email even more with a photo in it of a companion product that would go well with what they have already purchased. Above all, it is very handy for the customer if there is a direct link they can click on to the product to leave their review.

Another website I recently reviewed for someone had a coupon pop-up that offered 40% off immediately when the site opened. What does this say to consumers? It says that your items must already be marked up very high or you are desperate for sales. Unfortunately, this website owner was. They had raised all their prices to absorb the forty percent, but still no sales.

My advice was lower their prices to a reasonable level where they have room to occasionally offer 10-20 percent off items. There were other reasons they were not selling and it really had nothing to do with price. It had more to do with building desire through quality product photographs and descriptions. They also had no product reviews but because each piece was unique, that would not work well. In that case, a page dedicated to Raves/Reviews like we saw on Michelle's Vintage Jewelry would work great.

Navigation on your site is critical. Once people land there, they should be able to quickly click on items they are interested in. Product categories should be well-defined, along with your company policies, about us page, etc.

Many ecommerce sellers are currently using a very clean look and this is attractive. However, avoid being too drab. You want to create some excitement also about the site and your offerings. You will be able to change many things on your site's template including the background, header and footer colors; font size, type and color; button colors, and more. Experiment to get it looking the way you feel is most appealing.

If your site accommodates a rotating carousel, take advantage of that on your home page. It is easy to link each photo to the product so that customers are taken straight there. Here is how to do that:

Linking photos on carousel to product page:

First, go to the product matching the first photo on your carousel. At the top of your computer, highlight the URL, copy it

Go to the area where you uploaded the photo for the rotating carousel on your website. You will see a box where you can paste the URL of the product page. Then click save.

Repeat this for each photo on your carousel.

Once business pages are operational on Facebook, Twitter, Pinterest and other social networking sites, you will want to have icons on your home page linking to your business pages.

Showing somewhere on the home page (usually at the bottom) what type payment methods you accept is handy. You can also reiterate this in the message section on the home page, if desired.

If you have any trust seals or images, these are definitely things to have on that home page. This might include Paypal logos, trust seals for SSL through your credit card processor, Better Business Bureau symbols if you are a member, Google Trust seals, etc.

ACTION ITEMS:

- Start familiarizing yourself with the website theme layout you have chosen. If you run into difficulty or don't understand something, most of these web host providers have video tutorials to walk you through different processes.
- Upload your business logo and images to the header area of your website
- Obtain Google Voice or a toll-free number for your website. Place the number prominently on your homepage and again in the "contact us" area.
- Determine your shipping policies and put ship settings in place on website.
- Enable Product Reviews or install an available app for same on your site.
- Set up product categories, taking time to think of the most logical and easy sequence if you carry lots of variety
- Complete your "About Us" page for your site
- Experiment with background, header, footer colors on site as well as font styles and colors.
- Set up carousel images for home page if this is included with your website theme.

Although the action list is long this time, you will soon have a fully functioning, money making website. You are doing this! Truly, this is nose to the grindstone time.

NOTES:

Tracking People On Your Site

When you have created your website and have codes in place with Google Analytics, you will be able to see where your traffic is coming from. Charts will show you what pages they visit the most and even the amount of time spent on those pages. Along with your sales, this will assist you in knowing what marketing is working and what is not.

The use of Google Analytics does help you somewhat in search and it is a free tool. I would not create a website without it! Here is how to do it. First create a Google Analytics account (free). Go to: www.googleanalytics.com

If you already have a Gmail email address, use that to create the account. If you do not, you should find a checkbox that allows you to use your current email. As a side note, you may want to create a Gmail address to use for utilizing other Google related products that will be beneficial to you. These include Google+ which I write about in a later chapter.

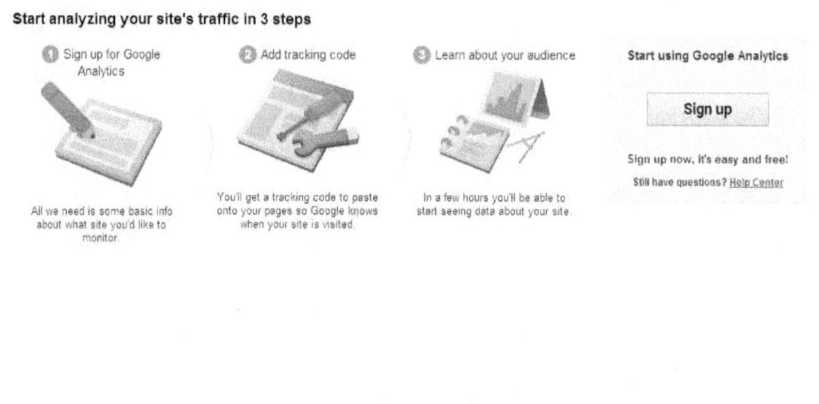

You will enter very little information to sign up but make sure what you enter is correct. It will ask you for the name of the website, URL, type of industry, and your time zone.

Google Analytics then has several check boxes to choose from regarding permissions, features and privacy. Once you complete those, click on Get Tracking ID at the bottom of the page.

As the next page comes up, look down toward the middle of it and you will see the tracking id number which generally starts with UA- followed by numbers. This number will be used to input into the background of your website to track visitor behavior.

Look at your website hosts help information to see where you will copy and paste this code as it is a different place on each hosting provider. If you have trouble, call them. They will help you do this one time set-up.

Google Analytics will help you somewhat in search and it may be something you learn a lot more about as time progresses. There is so much to learn about all the nuances of Google Analytics. Here is a link to a great blog that gives a ton of tips on the subject: http://gatipoftheday.com

You may also use Google Analytics to track what is happening with visitors on multiple sites including your pages on social networking sites.

For some of you, this may seem too technical. It is easier than you think. Google is doing all the work for you and all you have to do is log in occasionally and view on the charts and information to see what people are doing on any of your pages or sites you have set up. This information will assist you in knowing what is working and what is not. It gives you the opportunity to change your approach and capture more orders.

ACTION LIST:

- Sign up with Google Analytics
- Embed the code into your website in the appropriate place

The Direct Communicator

Some former and current eBay and Etsy users collect the email addresses of every customer they have sold to on those sites. For those that have not made a practice of this, you can pull all of those email addresses from Paypal for eBay customers. You can probably do this for the majority of them on Etsy also, though the site now offers additional payment plans.

For those who cry foul on this practice, I am going to point out that large retailers on eBay are doing the same thing for customer acquisition. It is likely that those big box and mid-size retailers you see on eBay use the site to acquire customers who they hope to have come to their site alone in the future. This technique and trend was recently reported in the 2015 State of Retailing Online report. See:

https://nrf.com/who-we-are/retail-communities/digital-retail-shoporg/state-of-retailing-online

If this does not sit right with you, start from square one and build your customer email list as you go along from those coming to your site and through social network marketing techniques. It is your choice how to proceed on this.

To be in compliance with ICANN, I carefully add customers to my email list using the following method.

First, I never place an eBay or Etsy packing slip in the order. The item is being shipped by my company that just happens to sell on eBay or Etsy. I insert my own professional invoice into their package that shows my website address, phone number, and gives them a coupon code or other incentive to visit my site.

Once I have shipped their order, I send the customer an email message from my company's email to their personal email (not through the eBay or Etsy platform) and let them know I appreciate their business. I give them their shipment tracking information. Again, I give them a link to my website and ask them if it is okay to send a monthly email to them with product news, sales, etc. Most people will gladly comply and I do promise that I will never send out mass emails to customers more than twice per month.

Each day I receive numerous emails from sites I have signed on with. Each day, they are deleted without even opening or reading them. I am sure you experience the same.

However, I have a few email subscriptions that I absolutely want to read. Here is what I notice about those emails. First, I am truly interested in the information they have to pass on. Second, they do not email so often. A monthly or bi-monthly email is more likely to be opened by me. For those reasons, I decided that my companies would only email periodically to our customers with the philosophy of less is more, as in more clicks and opens. Clicks and opens are more potential sales.

Sending a monthly newsletter or email message with current sales or new products is truly liquid gold! It does not take much time to reach many customers who have purchased from you before. These are the people most likely to purchase again.

Again, I do not send more than two emails per month to this list. I want them to be really interested when they receive it. If they are bombarded with too many emails, they tend to delete them or simply unsubscribe from the list, just like you or I may do.

A typical email that I send out would include news of any additional products we have added. It would have photos of those products. I may also include a coupon just for those customers to use for a limited time.

Further, the emails are targeted to certain segments of our clientele. Typical emails to customers are short, sweet and targeted. I recommend when you set up your email list that you include categories of interest. Your email communications will be more specific to your customers needs by utilizing this feature.

For instance, you may sell electronic products. What brand does your customer prefer? Are they an Apple or Android consumer? Let's say you sell bedding. What size bedding did they order? When you know if they have a queen, king, or California king preference, you can target those new sheets you are carrying that you picked up at a discount, but only in king size. You can then send a directed email to king size bedding buyers that is targeted and you will not be emailing everyone on your list, unless you choose to.

There are many great email program providers available. Many website hosting companies include an email list in your website platform of goodies. However, if you want to move into something larger with more features, take a look at some of these:

Mail Chimp – They have a free plan and you can also upgrade to a paid plan with more features and options. If you are just beginning, this may be a great choice for you.

Campaigner – I personally use this email program and love the reporting features and many templates. This service integrates with Google Analytics giving me further insight. I have no complaints about this service.

Constant Contact – highly recommended, used by many.

There are many more available. PC Magazine has prepared a nice side-by-side comparison of many email marketing software providers. See the 2015 article at:

http://www.pcmag.com/article2/0,2817,2453354,00.asp

Within many of these email program providers, you can do so many things. A/B split testing is very popular right now and here is how it works:

You are preparing to send a mass email to all of your 3200 customers. You want to see what email subject line would possibly get the most opens. A/B testing allows you to do this. Basically, your email system allows you to choose 2 different subject lines (or more) and then sends the two emails with the two separate subject lines to a few of your 3200 customers.

You could have one subject line that says:

"Terrific coupon savings plus new items" (subject line A)

The second test subject line could say:

"Hot new items with your bonus coupon" (subject line B)

Your email system sends the email to a select group of recipients (computer generated) and then it reports back to you with the stats on how many were opened, clicked on, etc.

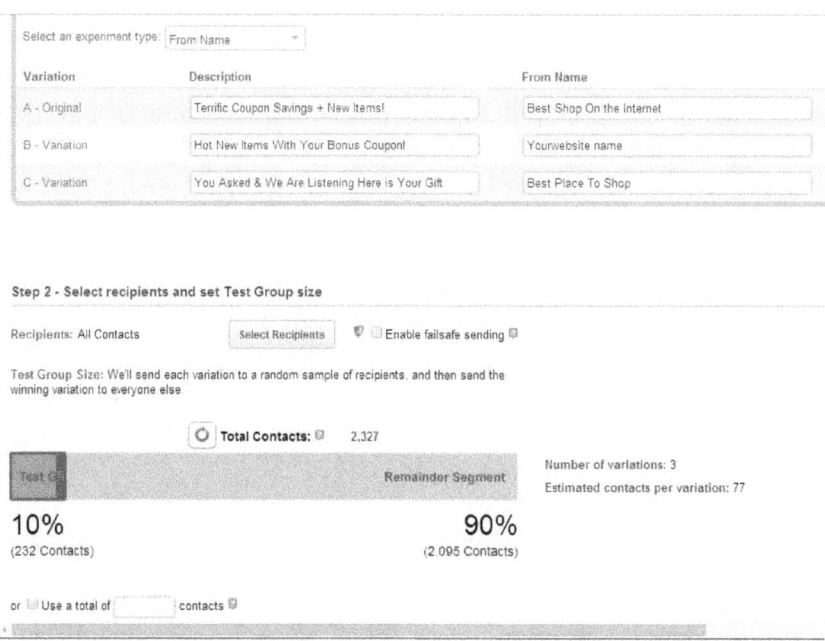

Once you see the results, send the winning subject line email to all the rest of your email list. Most programs allow you to allot a time period for how long you will do the testing. I normally choose 48 hours unless I am in a terrific hurry. Some people may not check their email for a couple of days.

In addition to experimenting with what is the most successful subject line, you may also experiment with the email address the message is coming from. For instance, you may have a general email address at Gmail that you experiment with one group and a website based email address such as info@yourdomain for the 2nd test.

With many email programs, you can select the size of the group you want to test, whether it is 10% of your email subscriber list or an exact number like 50 people.

Retargeting is another great feature to have in your email program. Once you have sent an email to your designated list, you can then have a special email that is sent only to those who have clicked on certain links within the email. For instance, you have just received an email from a vitamin company you have purchased from in the past. The email contains photos of two new products you are possibly interested in. You click one of the photos and proceed to be instantly taken to the website where you see more information about this item including its price. You are not sure you want to spend the money now.

On the other end, the email program is set to retarget you. It knows you clicked on that photo and it now sends another email to you offering a special buy one get one at half price coupon. The timing is also set by the operator of the email program to retarget you in one minute, one hour, or one day.

As consumers, we are often being retargeted. Remember that item you looked at on Amazon? Their system knows the day and time you looked at it and will send you a follow-up email asking if you are still interested in it or that it is now on sale. You can do that also by enabling certain features on your newly created Google Analytics account. This is what is happening when you surf the web and that dress you saw at a particular site keeps popping up as an advertisement asking if you are still interested.

With an effective email program, you can have that same sort of retargeting power. It just takes some time to learn it and set things into place. All of this may sound like trouble, but these tools are in place for you to be more successful at what you do and have more sales.

In the beginning, if you want to just stick to creating your email database and sending an email every couple of weeks or on holidays, this is fine. Keep things simple in the beginning and then work your way into these other options as you go along with building your brand and online store.

Remember that A/B split testing is an important component to see what gives you the most opens. Keep it enticing, but real. Do not be tempted to create an outrageous subject line to just get opens and then have a customer disappointed at what they find. That will drive them away from your company.

Retargeting is an essential component in driving more sales. Remember, people must often see something two, three or even four times before they pull the trigger and purchase. This is why we see advertisements over and over again.

Finally, there has been much research conducted on the best time to send emails. Currently it appears to be Tuesdays. I usually send my emails out on Tuesday or Wednesday. Being on Eastern Standard Time, I choose to have the emails sent in the afternoon. Early on I found that many subscribers unsubscribed from the list when I was sending it out at 8 or 9am EST. Most had opened the email via their mobile device. This tells me that people don't like seeing emails early in the morning. They are still waking up or getting ready for their day and consider it a nuisance.

I find that when the majority of them are hitting the mid-day doldrums, this is the best time to send my emails. Remember when you schedule the email to be aware of people in other time zones. Will it be morning there? Obviously if you have a lot of international customers, this can be difficult. I happen to keep a checkbox on my email program that categorizes my international customers. I can then choose a different time to send them the same email.

It is wise to go ahead and start setting dates for having important email events scheduled. These could be Cyber Monday, holiday events, etc. By working on these email templates prior to the date they will arrive in your customer's email box, you will save yourself a lot of last minute stress. Many ecommerce merchants begin working on their 4th quarter season in July to August of each year.

When you are setting up your email program, I would encourage you to make categories or lists of your customers based on what area of the world they live in, what they have purchased, future possible product interests, etc.

Most marketing gurus agree that email is still the king when it comes to having an effective program for driving sales at your website. Start here and then build your online social presence which we will cover next.

ACTION LIST:

- Gather up your customer email list and import it into your new email program of choice if you are not already using one.
- Start designing your first email to this list, maybe an announcement of the new site. Schedule your email into the future when your site is live and ready for visitors.
- Create a schedule on your calendar to send 2 emails to this list per month. You can send more, but I would not bombard those on the list.
- Make a list of important annual emails to send such as Cyber Monday Sales, Holiday Sales, Small Business Saturday, etc. Begin crafting those emails in advance so you are ready and not trying to compose them during times of high stress.

Most email providers can import your email list using several different file formats. Check with them first. Consider sending a first email to your customers announcing your new site and maybe featuring a new or popular product. Once you read about content marketing in an upcoming chapter, we will talk about how important that is to include in email marketing.

NOTES:

Finding Your Customers

You are an internet retailer and never has it been so easy to reach people worldwide with your wares! Social networking sites (SNS) are critical to expand your outreach and much of it is free or costs very little for the return on investment (ROI).

If you believe that sites such as Facebook and Twitter are only for those people posting "selfies" and random quotes and such, you would be missing out. These sites give your business the opportunity to get social with current and future customers. It is measured by the term *engagement*. How many followers on sites engaged with your post, advertisement or message is what this term measures.

The numbers are growing each year exponentially. Currently over 60% of Twitter users have purchased through links on the site. Facebook continues to drive sales also and is essentially the leader of the pack statistically. However, this can be different for each business. Currently, I have to say that Pinterest is driving many sales for my two sites and this has cost me nothing! Yet, I also place targeted ads on Facebook and have had tremendous results. I will show you some examples in upcoming pages.

Social networking sites allow us to find our customers and where they hang out. Whether it is Instagram, Pinterest, Youtube or the other players, this is where you will find the people who want your products.

You want to leverage as many of these sites as possible for your business because you do not yet know exactly where your customers are hanging out online. Many of them will primarily be on one site, while you have the opportunity to pick up say 10% more on another SNS.

Due to the fact that you have so much to do to get your website up and running, you may want to just focus on two or three during the first few weeks. Consider scheduling to add another SNS every so often until you have a business presence on each one. They are all different and you will need a little time with each one to see its inner workings.

I am also going to tell you about easy to use apps that can automate much of this for you. These applications are like hiring an employee for $10-$25 per month. Yes, per month not day or hour.

As you read about each social networking site and join under your business name, keep in mind that people are there to engage socially, not purchase products. They don't mind liking certain businesses, but they want to choose and do not want to be bombarded with constant product posts only. You should sprinkle in other items of interest to them. This could include funny photos, cute animals or children, news that may be relevant to them, etc. Never be political or overly opinionated with your posts as to not offend some potential or current customers.

I want to stress that the key to getting buying customers to your website is finding where they hang out online. Social networking sites provide you with that opportunity. So, let's get social with your business!

Winning at Pinning

This site has been a very real resource for driving traffic to my websites. I cannot tell you how many phone calls I have had from customers who originally found one of the products I offer on Pinterest.

A recent conversation with a customer went like this:

"Hello, I saw your shoes on Pinterest, well actually I was looking up a recipe, and then I saw your shoes and I've got to have them. I see you are out of my size. When will you have more?"

I paid nothing for this marketing! Most of my sales that began from Pinterest have been free. Recently, I have begun promoting a few select pins and it is pennies I am paying, not a lot of money for the exposure and much less than I have paid to Google Adwords in the past.

Create a free business account on Pinterest if you do not already have one and pin all of your products onto the site. Follow people and get followers. Make it real and genuine – follow others whose photos or products you like. Make different boards to categorize things.

For instance, let's say you sell camera equipment. You could create several boards and set them up like this:

Portraits – Black & White

Portraits – Color

Landscapes – Black & White

Nature – Color

Vintage Photo Equipment

Cool Lenses

Special Effects

Best Cameras

Best Lenses

Best Filters

Along with pinning photos you find that are already on Pinterest to those boards, also pin photos of your products that are linked to your website.

Once your website is up, this is so easy to do. Just pull up your product page on your website (in customer mode), and click the Pinterest button to share that item. Make sure to have your website linked!

There are people who will pin for you for a small fee. I have never used another person as it can all be done very quickly. As stated earlier, you can also sign up with Pinterest to promote select product pins. This is a recent addition to Pinterest to have the choice of paying to have your pins promoted.

I have made numerous boards on Pinterest and have what I consider a modest following now on the site (under 1000). Still, a large amount of business comes from Pinterest because other people are always re-pinning your pins. They may not follow you now or will never follow you, but your pins are still making it around the site for others to see and click on. This is free! You are getting free advertising each time people are doing this. This is like having an army of people showing your products to others for absolutely nothing!

Some of the boards I make have nothing to do with my business, but they assist me in targeting people who may like my products. For instance, I created a Castle board with beautiful pins of castles. I found all of the photos of the castles on Pinterest. One of the items I sell is costumes and I will pin costumes related to the medieval time period within those boards. People who are following the castle board will see the costumes in their feed, along with the beautiful photos of castles.

Get started with Pinterest right away. It is fun and they have a great mobile app that is free. You can pin on your phone when you are doing something mundane or boring.

If you are utilizing Shopify as your website host, they have a new feature which allows you to have every product automatically uploaded to Pinterest with buy buttons. One caveat is that you have to be approved. Your store must have a certain number of successful sales prior to approval. This is an invaluable tool, however, if you are on the Shopify platform.

Like most social media sites, Pinterest is evolving and I really like what it is becoming. Their numbers show that Pinterest users are much more likely to make online purchases.

ACTION ITEMS:

- Set up business account at www.pinterest.com
- Start Pinning but do it in as described.
- Please go to my website and also sign up for my free list of Powerful Pinning Techniques that will bring you even more revenue. Also, I have included complete instructions for linking Pinterest to your business website so that you may be approved as a business with them. www.karenfielden.com

A Little Bluebird Told Me

Many business owners cannot sing enough praise about this social site. It's hard to believe all those little tweets can turn into money in your pocket. Make it a priority to start learning Twitter as soon as you can.

Create a free business page on Twitter with the same name as your website. If your site is GeraldinesGoodies.com – name your Twitter account Geraldine's Goodies. The site will ask for your full name. Again, put your company name, company email address and company phone.

Set up your profile page with your company logo and a wide header photo at the top of your page that shows your brand, products, both or more.

Choose one of Twitter's theme colors for your profile and put in your company name in the appropriate section along with details about what you sale. Condense, as space is limited on Twitter. Put your website URL along with your location which could be broad like USA, Canada, UK or Australia.

Once your profile is complete and you have clicked save, you will see suggestions for people to follow. Generally, these are very popular celebrities who have a huge following. Go to the search bar and find celebrities or companies with huge followings in your industry. Here is an example:

You sell auto parts. Search for Counting Cars, the show on the History Channel. Search for individuals on the show. Follow them. They probably will not follow you back, but they might. They may even purchase some auto parts from you in the future. The reason you are doing this is because Twitter will match up possible persons for you to follow with the kind of people you are following. Since Twitter is performing this action based upon interests, it makes sense for you to keep within people and companies related to your industry. Another example would be to perform a search on Twitter for auto restoration and see who you could follow related to that. You get the idea.

What if you sell shoes? Search for the brand names first of the companies you sell. Follow them. Next, search keywords on Twitter such as work boots, snow boots, tennis shoes, sneakers, high heels, stilettos, etc. Follow related companies and people that appear. Which celebrities wear the types of shoes you sell?

Try to post or tweet on Twitter at least once daily. Again, I will tell you about some apps that do this for you shortly. Be aware that posts are limited on Twitter to 140 spaces or characters. Remember to add a few "hashtags". This is always difficult for me to remember for some reason. I often make posts and forget the hashtags but go back in and edit to add them.

Make your posts relevant to what may interest a potential customer. Again using auto parts, you could tweet stating which parts people request the most (fenders, alternators, etc.) and that you have parts for almost all vehicles. Don't know what to post on a particular day? You could just tweet "Remember, we ship your auto parts fast" or "We ship auto parts worldwide". Use hash tags at the end of your tweet. #fenders #alternators #auto parts. Of course, make sure there is a link to your site.

Hashtags greatly increase your exposure across the internet. They assist in organizing subjects such as homemade bread, Caribbean, lighthouses, gifts, photos, binders, books, etc., so that they appear in the feed of various social networking platforms and searches. This helps you find those interested in what you offer. That is our entire goal: finding where your customers hang out.

If you can upload a photo with your tweet this is often more effective. There are so many tweets going on, it is impossible not to scroll past many of them and not read them. A great photo about your product or topic will peak interest.

Once you have gathered a following, use tweets to ask questions and engage socially. In September, I tweeted that Halloween is on Friday this year. Think of all the parties. How soon do you start getting ready? Your site URL #Halloween #costumes

I have never purchased advertising on Twitter so I cannot comment on its effectiveness. I have less experience on Twitter than I do Facebook or Pinterest. However, I have recently amped up my presence on the site with the help of apps.

I see that a little time spent on Twitter a few times per week is good for my business and building followers and rapport. In fact, I have found it easy to get followers on Twitter. I spend that time reposting tweets from others following me and comment on their posts. Twitter is a place where you need to engage with them also to reap rewards.

Changing The Face of Business

If there is one site that has truly changed the way we do business, it is Facebook. From Proctor & Gamble to small little niche websites, this venue has so much to offer any business if you use it correctly.

To create a page for your business, you use a different button than the one to create an account for an individual. If you look at the bottom right of the main Facebook login page, you will see "Create a page for a band, celebrity or business". That is where you want to click for the page creation for your website's presence on Facebook.

Once you are at the next screen, choose "Brand or Product" and the appropriate category if you are an online store only. If you also have a brick and mortar store, choose "Local Business or Place".

During the creation of your company's Facebook page, you can upload your company logo in the same place you would normally put a personal photo, if desired. You can upload a screenshot of your website's home page in the "cover" area – or a photo of your inventory (if attractive). You might also use a stitch feature with photo software such as Picasa and blend 3-4 of your most popular products. Use your imagination and make it fun. This is true also for the cover area of your profile on many social networking sites.

Keep in mind that as you post on Facebook with your business page, only those persons who have "liked" your page will see the posts. I started out with my own friends. Yes, I hounded them to "like" my new Facebook business page. Most of them obliged. This gave me some followers instead of none.

I also utilized my email list. Facebook will take your email list and try to find everyone on it for you. You can then send them an invite to like your business page.

Next, I utilized Facebook's advertising. I now have well over 6000 followers for one business page, but less for another business page which I am working more now.

Just like with Pinterest and Twitter, it is good to post something daily on your Facebook page. It can be as simple as "We are now shipping lots of adorable plush sea turtles. Get yours now" with a link and product photo.

The key is consistency. If you drop off the radar of the people who have liked you, it is difficult to get back on it with Facebook. They use a type of algorithm that keeps posts hidden that people are not engaging with very often.

Remember: this is free. Yes, it does require effort and time, but it can hardly be called work. You're looking at future dollars for spending a little time posting on Facebook. Most of your friends and relatives are just spending time on the site and will see no money from their time spent. You are so smart! Read the Applications chapter in this book and see how you can get an app that will do this for you very cost effectively.

You will receive an email from Facebook periodically telling how many people have engaged with your page and other interesting stats. In the beginning, I really was not sure how to interpret this information. Over time, I have learned the jargon and you will as well.

I have had great success with Facebook paid advertising. It has assisted me with building a decent size following of over 6000 truly interested consumers instead of just "likes" that turn into no sales. Facebook ads have shown actual sales results for me.

Once you have created your Facebook business page, you will see a box to the right that says "Promote Your Page". Currently, you will see two options there: Promote your website or promote your Facebook page. Choose one of them.

The next box that pops up will allow you to enter the text you want to appear to people on Facebook. It will also allow you to choose what types of people are going to see this advertisement. Select the gender that will see it, age group, and most importantly, things they are interested in. Your selections on this are experimental at this point, yet important. Think of who buys your products. What are there other interests? Facebook will assist you as you type in a particular phrase like custom autos, it will self generate other close topics. Choose several of them.

Set a budget as low as $5.00 for your ad to run and spread it out over 3-4 days if possible. Facebook requires you to spend at least $1 per day.

Let's say you sell infant apparel. Under "Interests", you would type in the keywords baby, infants, baby clothing, toddler, etc. Once you start typing this in, Facebook will offer more targeting suggestions.

Facebook has collected a vast amount of information on people and what interests them. It is important to precision target your future customers using this feature under the Interest section.

Note that you can also target specific countries. If you are in Canada and only want USA and Canada customers, this would be the place to designate that.

When you are ready to advertise on Facebook, put your best product out there. Make sure it is not common unless you have a blow out price on it.

Here is a screenshot of results from an ad I spent $8.00 on in April 2015. The ad had a photo of a well dressed vampire. The caption said, "Every girl's crazy about a sharp dressed vampire". Be aware that it did not even feature a product I sell, but it made buyers like my Facebook page, visit my website and resulted in sales.

I targeted the ad to specific groups. The ad ran for four days so I spent $2 per day.

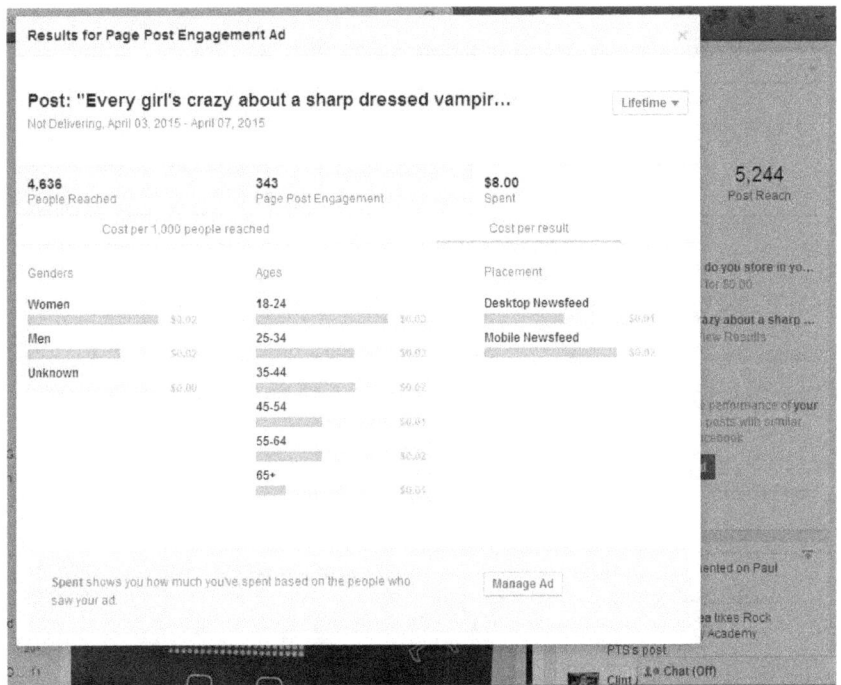

Over 4,600 persons were reached with this advertisement. You can see the graphs for age and gender demographics, as well as whether they viewed it on a desktop or mobile device. We also see the cost per 1000 people reached and it averages around 2 cents, an incredibly low figure.

There were 343 page post engagements. This means that there were 343 actions by those advertised to with the post. Facebook breaks down many of these actions for you in their reporting features as shown below.

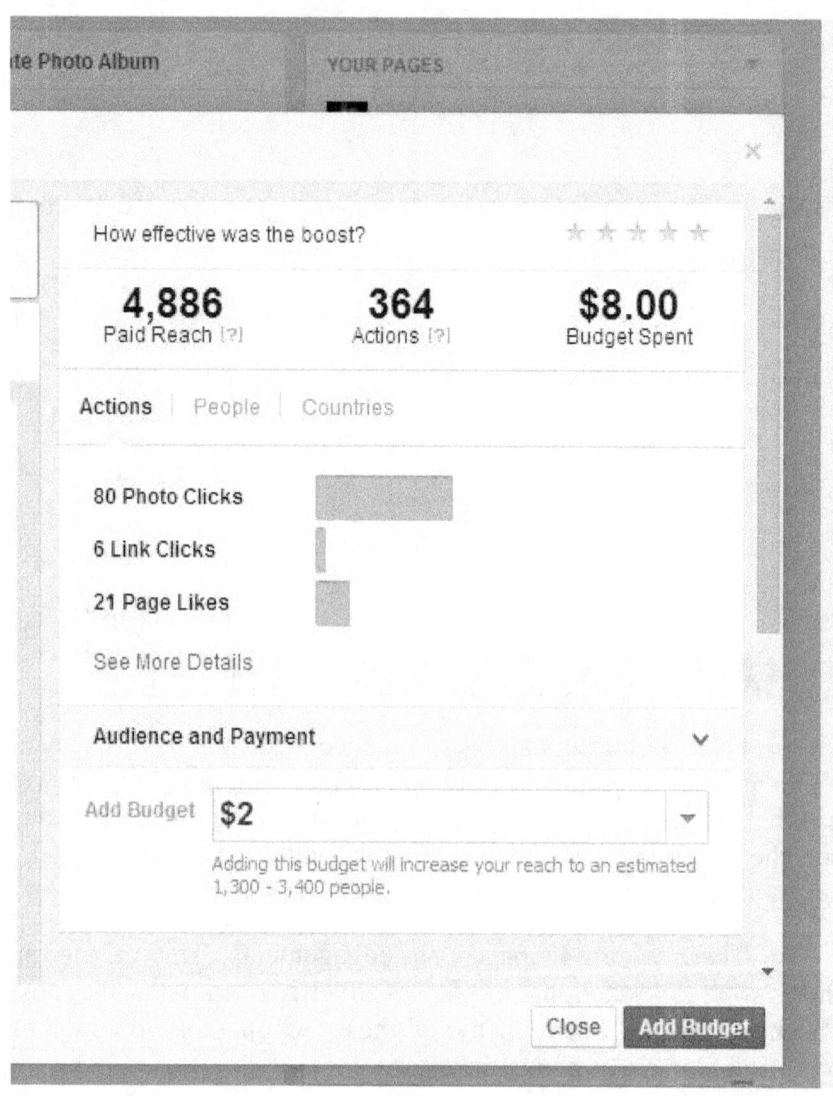

How effective was the boost?

★ ★ ★ ★ ★

4,886
Paid Reach [?]

364
Actions [?]

$8.00
Budget Spent

Actions | People | Countries

80 Photo Clicks

6 Link Clicks

21 Page Likes

See More Details

Audience and Payment

Add Budget | **$2**

Adding this budget will increase your reach to an estimated 1,300 - 3,400 people.

Close | **Add Budget**

The 80 photo clicks took the customer straight to our website. The 6 link clicks did the same. We received 21 new page likes.

What is really a bonus is that this same ad actually had an even larger reach. That is because when this report was run, the same post was still receiving likes, shares, and clicks even though the advertising campaign had ended. This is achievable due to the fact that people are still out there on Facebook sharing the post with each other.

$8.00 is a small amount to spend and it did result in three sales which netted well above the $8.00 spent. This is just one successful advertisement on Facebook. I have many more that had even more dramatic results.

Is it coming together for you? Are you realizing that you really can afford to advertise your business and drive sales for a nominal amount?

The key to finding the people who are going to buy your products is letting them find you. You must hang where they hang. Utilizing targeted audience marketing on all social sites is the key that unlocks the door to you and your customer meeting and saying "Hello". You cannot just "willy nilly" place an ad on Facebook and get good results. Use the power of Facebook's vast information collected on people to find your customers.

Take advantage of another free gift to you. Download ***Facebook Success Plan for Business*** at my website www.karenfielden.com

Photographs Equal Money

For the first few months on Instagram, I really did not have a clue what the site held for me in the way of business. I knew that it was a site where people did not want to constantly be "sold" something. I knew it was a place where every post had to have a photo. I knew hashtags were important along with linking any product photos to my website. But, I did not know what I was doing.

Finally, I discovered that Instagram is purely a content marketing platform when applied to business. Now owned by Facebook, it can be used in a number of ways. First, it is a visual platform with little text on posts. This is the perfect place for great photos and videos. People respond much more to images and their brains process that information much faster than text. You could fill up your website or blog with tons of text explaining your product benefits. Yet, a picture is truly worth a thousand words or more.

One feature, Instagram Direct, is where you may privately interact with others. This can be used to target people following you who like or engage with your posts the most. For follow-up customer service and retention, you could send a thank you the same way. Instagram is all about a photo so each time you send one of these private messages, you would send a photo with it, for instance a big thank you picture or whatever you can imagine.

In the beginning of Instagram, all photos had to be square. Now, the site has changed to include many shapes including panoramic. Do not forget that videos are also often shared. What if you created a video thank you showing you and your staff to send to customers?

Instagram recently introduced its own app for iPhone and iPad users called Hyperlapse. This is an incredible app that allows for time lapse video. It turns your normal videos into a unique visual experience. They are working on developing an android version also. Watch a demo here: https://vimeo.com/104410054

With over 200 million Instagram users of which over 100 million access the site daily, there is an incredible opportunity here for businesses to be social with their existing customers and make new ones. Although Twitter is limited in the amount of text each post can contains, you can post up to thirty hashtags on Instagram, thus covering a huge spectrum of subjects that can relate to your post.

It is important to post on all social sites in a way that says you are not only about pushing your product or company. To engage your audience, try posting funny cartoons, great quotes, news in your industry, customer stories, videos, etc. I generally post 2 items that are not my products, but something I believe will interest the followers, and then a product. That 2:1 ratio seems to work well for me, but follow your own experimentation with this. The overall message here is that people do not want to constantly be hounded with sales pitches, but they will engage if you keep things interesting, newsworthy, relative and fun.

On Instagram, each post must contain a picture. Get creative here with scenes at your office, even if it is a home office. Show orders being packed and send out a thank you thumbs up message. When another Instagram user likes one of your product photos you posted, use the private message feature to engage with them. You could say: "thanks for liking _____. We have a lot of happy customers using this item. I wanted to offer you 10% off. Use coupon code: _____ at our website on anything you like! Your code is valid for ___ days. Cheers"

These are just a few ideas. Indeed, there are books on the subject of each of these individual social platforms. Be creative, test, and use analytical tools to track what gets your best responses. To get ideas of how other companies are using any of the social sites, watch what they are doing and look at the quality of their posts. Follow Wal-Mart and Target. They are doing a great job on this site.

To sign up for Instagram, you must download the free app to your smart phone. This is where you have to create your user account. Once your account is established, you may also use your computer to log in and view your photos.

Using apps, you can also stream Instagram to show up on your website. There are many sites that do a great job featuring this. Take a look at Black Milk Clothing from Australia on Instagram. With over one million followers, they claim to have never paid for advertising, at least in the beginning. The start-up company quickly rose to fame from Instagram postings. www.blackmilkclothing.com

Linking It All Together

Linkedin is a platform I began using later on. There are many uses for it and you will find numerous business resources on the site within groups that can assist you in expanding as an entrepreneur.

Develop a profile for yourself as the owner, founder or whatever title you designate for your company. Link your website. As with prior social networking sites, invite your email list to link with others. Join groups that are in your interest categories.

Talk about your products. Make sure to post a link to your website. You can include verbiage in your bio about how you became interested in these products or developed them yourself. Basically, you want to cover the W's – Who you are – Why you do it – What you do – Where you are located, etc.

Linkedin is about building relationships online. There are over 300 million users of this site. You have the opportunity to let people know who you are, what you sell, offer them advice on those products and build friendships.

As an author, I can let fellow members know what books I have written, what I am working on, post questions and surveys asking what their current challenges are in their business.

Depending upon the types of products you sell, you have the chance to network with like-minded individuals. You may find yourself inspired by a new idea for your business posted by another member.

While maybe not as critical as your business pages on Facebook, Twitter or Pinterest, Linkedin is yet another avenue for you to be social and expand your brand, reach and sales.

Your blog posts should always be re-posted to your Linkedin page. This shows you know your industry and gives relevant, interesting or entertaining information.

Linkedin can become a tremendous resource for you in that you may have a follower who collects art glass and you just happen to sell it. You may be in the apparel industry and come across a great supplier you did not know of before. You may decide at some point that you would like to sell your business and find an interested party on this site. The networking possibilities are endless.

You and The Tube

No matter what you sell, you can utilize the power of Youtube for free. In addition to video, did you know you can make product photo slide shows with or without music on Youtube? I have used this feature when I did not have video and analytics shows traffic to my website from this source.

Again, create your Youtube account under your business name that is the same as your website name, keeping your brand consistent. If you have already created a Gmail account, it will be simple to set up the Youtube account.

I was astounded to read that Youtube is now the number two search engine right behind Google. This news makes it a sales avenue not to be ignored for your business. Source: http://www.hubspot.com/marketing-statistics

Unlike Pinterest, Facebook, Twitter and Instagram, uploads on Youtube can comfortably be only about your product or services, unless you want to do something else creative with it. Youtube viewers are more receptive to products. They are just looking to see how you feature those products in your postings.

A company called Vat19 does a fantastic job with their Youtube channel from the way it is laid out to the videos they upload. Take a look at https://www.youtube.com/user/vat19com After viewing their videos, it is easy to assume that Youtube has significantly bumped their sales and customer database list.

You can use videos or still photo slideshows to demonstrate how a product is used and address some of those questions people tend to have once they receive it. These videos can also be embedded into your website right on each product page. Videos showing how the customer will have fun with, benefit from, or love using your product work to increase sales.

When you upload your video or still photos to Youtube, there will be a section to enter keywords. Make sure you use this section and insert any keywords relevant to your video.

For example, you have made a video showing how easy it is to use the tile cleaning solution you sell and how it is earth-friendly, bio-degradable, safe for humans and pets, etc. Keywords to include would be:

Cleaning Tile

Safe Home Cleaning

Pet Safe Cleaning

Earth Friendly Cleaning

Bio-degradable Cleaners

Just like hashtags, these keywords boost you tremendously as people search the internet. Your video will be viewed many more times as a result than if you had no keywords.

Action List:

- Keep a page in your business binder or notebook with ideas for videos to implement soon.
- Schedule a time in the future when you can begin to make your first video to upload to Youtube. Check out other resources on the internet for doing so if you are a beginner. With kids uploading all kinds of videos that become viral, you can do this too.

With a little creativity, you can take your business from sleepy to fully awake and shipping out lots of orders with the power of Youtube.

Google+ (Google Plus)

Take advantage of another free spot on the internet that assists you in getting indexed by Google search engines. Less than 15% of company brands post content on Google+ more than three times per week. Those that do post often, have a greater chance of driving traffic to their websites.

What is Google+? This is Google's version of social networking. It is included with your Gmail account. There is a feature you can click on that takes you to an area where you may set up your Google+ account.

While logged into Gmail, click on the 9 dotted icon just to the right of the word Images shown in the picture below. It will then bring up other Google products. Click on the G+ red button bottom left corner and proceed to set up your Google+ business page.

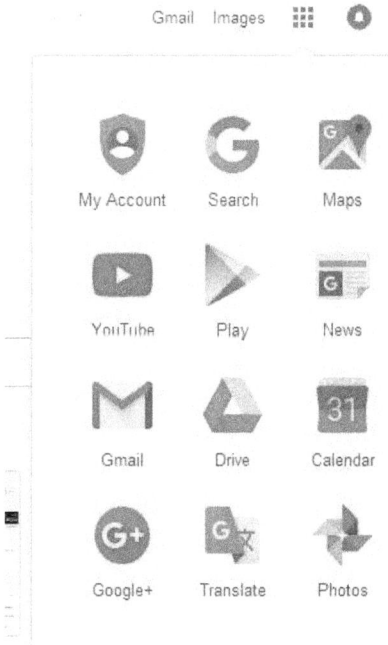

Of course, by now you are quite adept at uploading your logo, header images and more. The great news is you only have to do this once on all these sites unless you decide to change the look of your branding.

Google+ allows for uploads of very high resolution photos without changing the quality of them. This is true for videos also. Video users may participate together on Google Hangouts. This is a bit like Skype and I believe you may be able to record the call also, if desired. I have not used Google Hangouts but will try it in the near future.

I have been more focused on Google+ because of the flexibility I have of copying and pasting relative material from my blog to the site and connecting with customers who use Gmail. I also believe that participating in Google+ assists in search for my brands.

Knowing how Google operates, there will be many more features added in the future as they are constantly innovating.

Works Like The Energizer Bunny

What is all this talk about blogs and why do you need one? Blogs are like a tireless system that fetches customers for you. They keep working without a change of batteries. A blog post that generates interest gets customers to you and your products. It creates a yellow brick road that brings Dorothy and her friends to your doorstep, even though they were looking for something else.

There are two main steps to blogging. First, you or someone else will write the blog and insert great photographs, graphics, and/or video. Second, you will post the blog to generate interest and activity in several sites across the internet that we have talked about earlier.

The blog should post to every social site you are on including Instagram with a photo from the blog. It should be included on your Linkedin account. If you have a video with the blog, that should, of course, connect to Youtube. Finally, you may include a link to the blog with a teaser line in one of your bi-monthly emails you are sending out.

The most effective blogs do not just give regular product news. They utilize content marketing which is information of value in exchange for showcasing your company and its wares.

One example of content marketing might be a blog post on "The contest for the best baby diapers is over!" If you sell infant items, you will have a post that tells about your experience with different diaper brands, cloth diapers, innovations, and your final favorite choice. As the reader of your post can see from where they have landed, you also sell really neat items for babies. Here are possible actions that can happen with each person that reads the blog:

Read it and never return

Sign up to stay informed

See an item and put it in their shopping cart and leave

See an item and purchase it right then

Share/Post the article to a social site

Send a product link to a friend/relative

I try to make a blog post on my sites at least two times per week. If you feel your writing skills are too weak, hire someone you know or look online for a skilled ghost writer for your blog posts. Another idea is to hire an intern at a local college or even a high school senior who is very good at writing and may have their own blog.

Since I blog often, I alternate a combination of company and product news in some posts, along with content marketing blog posts. You can only promote your "about us" page so many times, A fresh blog is something new to share within your marketing bundle you are putting together.

Another idea is to use video in your posts. The writing you then do is very limited, usually a headline. Use your video to show your products, how to use them, etc. This is also known as a Vlog.

Generally, you do not get quick sales or results with blogs. However, do not overlook this gem in your arsenal of marketing weapons. Blogging is something that must be done consistently because it builds your brand, brings you to the forefront as an authority on lamps, lingerie, antiques or whatever you sell.

Content marketing comes alive with blogging. How-to's are very popular. Blogs are read, shared and passed around the internet and definitely searchable. Having a blog gives you more credibility as a business. Of course, blogs always lead to your main product site.

The most shared posts are those that you can learn something from or gain value in some way. If you sell cosmetics that are all natural with no animal testing, you may want to write a content centered blog about the most beneficial natural ingredients to look for in skin care.

Some examples of content marketing include sharing information on:

Product How to use - How to choose the correct size – Celebrities who are wearing/using your product - Unique ways to – Checklist for -

New products and company news are important also, but they do not really qualify as content marketing. It is critical that you make content marketing one of your ninja tasks! I think I just heard a loud whining noise. Even if you do not feel qualified, make an attempt, you may surprise yourself.

Can you make a checklist related to products you sale, but not about those items? For instance if you sell silk flowers, write a *Top Ten Ways To Keep Your Silk Flowers Fabulous* blog. Go to a site like canva.com where you can make a graphic for free. Use that graphic to pin with links and hashtags to Pinterest and other social sites. Now, you are attracting people who have an interest in silk flowers by the graphic that leads people to your blog which is, of course, connected to your site.

Go to Pinterest.com and type in the search bar: 5 makeup tips for older women. Click on the match that appears and you will probably see a link to Cindy Joseph's website. This is a great example of content marketing. Cindy is doing a terrific job taking care of a huge population of female baby boomers. She uses photos, videos and more to sell herself and her products.

Inserting product photos or any photograph or video that drives home a point and relates to your topic is always desired in blogs. Be sure to make the blog visual and not just text.

You will want to use tags in your blog. There is an appropriate box or section for this on all blog formats. You may also use hashtags. What is the difference?

First, tags are like hashtags but do not have the #. Hashtags tend to be trendy or even a fad and will fade in internet popularity. Tags live longer with search engines. This does not devalue hashtag use on social platforms. That is where they are given the cue with the "#" symbol that all of these social posts line up on that subject.

It sounds complicated and it is confusing. Just remember to use hashtags on Twitter, Facebook, Instagram and Pinterest. Use keywords on Youtube. Use tags on your blogs.

You do not need to write a full feature magazine article. In fact, your blog post should be easy to read and not too long. People are busy and they want information quickly. The more visual your blog is with photos, graphs, and videos, the more effective it will probably be.

While there are many successful businesses that have never incorporated a blog, they may have other elements going on that you are not aware of to capture new business. Many of them may have firmly established their brand and customer base prior to vast use of the internet and the invention of the "blog".

Occasionally, I purchase items from Bissell, a cleaning company that has been around a long time. They do not have a blog, but they do have several other elements that may fit into your website, depending upon your niche. The first thing I notice is the Ask an Expert section. Here you can find people writing in to ask how to remove certain stains or take care of particular cleaning issues. Those questions could also have been common questions the company receives and want to address for the masses. Taken to the next level with social network marketing, all of those subjects the company has posted could definitely qualify as content marketing. Further, they establish Bissell as an expert.

I also found of interest the how-to videos on product usage. Again, all of those videos can be posted on Pinterest, Youtube and many other sites. See: www.bissell.com

According to an in depth article on blogging by Yahoo Small Business,

81% of US consumers trust information from blogs

61% of consumers have made a purchase based on recommendations from a blog

The average person watches 182 online videos per month

Small businesses that blog receive 126% more lead growth than businesses who do not have a blog.

Source: https://smallbusiness.yahoo.com/advisor/top-blogging-statistics-45-reasons-blog-180101993.html

There are many interesting statistics dealing with everything we have been talking about you implementing with your business in that article. I recommend it. This is why I have stressed that blogging is essential to building your customer base.

It may seem like a big deal to regularly write a blog or to pay someone else to do it, but this one advertising resource will not just sit on "your blog". You will copy and paste it to Tumbler and Google+. It will be tweeted and posted on Facebook. Your visual with the link can go to Instagram and Pinterest. Plus, there are even more sites to paste your blog and its associated images if you want. You get a lot of traction out of the blog! Just remember that expanding your reach and bringing new customers to your site without paying for advertising is accomplished through content marketing.

Paying Per Click

Google Adwords is the advertising program that fuels the massive search engine. Granted, Google pulls information from all over the internet. However, your competitors who are paying for Google Adwords will generally show up before you do in searches.

Up to this time, we have worked on spreading your presence all over the internet using social networking platforms, Youtube and blogs. We have covered low cost ways to grow your business. Many people do one of two things to advertise their business: 1) they spend most of their budget if not all of on Google Adwords; 2) they spending nothing on Adwords out of fear of being able to control their ads and the cost.

I believe you can get results with Google Adwords on a small budget of say $25.00 per month. In addition, almost every website host includes $75 - $100 in free Adwords advertising with your site. Make sure you take advantage of that.

You do not have to be locked into any type of long contract to use Google Adwords. I may start an advertising campaign with them and then pause it for awhile if I feel it is not producing results that I want. This pause feature gives me time to look at keywords and change my approach. I can tweak the ads I have running or I can begin a different advertising campaign to see if that brings better results.

Keywords drive this type of advertising. What is your product niche? These are the keywords you want to use for advertising campaigns. You may want to look at any research you did with Google Trends for your products to see what are the most search for words or terms. What is trending in your category?

For instance, you may sell Christmas décor and right now people are searching for fiber optic trees over artificial trees. They may also be searching for flocked artificial Christmas trees.

Here is another ninja tip. Use the site www.spyfu.com to see how your competitors rank in search and what keywords they are using the most. Spyfu is a very resourceful tool that has a paid platform. However, once you get past the introductory video on the home page, you can type in a competitor's website URL and get really great relevant information on the top four or five. You may also click up in the right hand corner to save the information as a pdf emailed to you. You may find that this really helps direct you on coming up with keywords for your advertising and negative keywords as well.

Negative keywords should be included in your Adwords account so that you do not have people clicking your ads that are looking for something other than what you are offering.

For instance if you sell pre-owned and vintage military uniforms and equipment, your keywords for your advertising might be:

Vintage Military Goods – Vintage Military Uniforms – Military Uniforms, etc.

Your negative keywords might be:

Careers – Education – Jobs – Vehicles

You are not offering information on military careers, education, jobs or vehicles and you do not want to pay for those clicks.

Here is an excellent article from Adstage by Sam Mazaheri with many different negative keywords to choose from.

http://www.techwyse.com/blog/pay-per-click-marketing/75-negative-keywords-that-every-adwords-campaign-should-include/

Keep your Google Adwords budget small in the beginning and just experiment with different keywords and watch results. It is easy to track in real time what people are responding to. You will see this information on your Google Adwords page.

To sign up for this advertising, just go to:

http://www.google.com/adwords

Sign up using your company Gmail account you (hopefully) created. Before you begin placing advertisements, you will be asked for a credit or debit card to keep on file for payment. Unlike Facebook, you only pay for clicks also known as pay per click (ppc). You may also decide how much you want to pay per click. You can pay as little as one cent per click.

ACTION LIST

- Set up Google Adwords Account
- Make sure to enter any coupon codes you have from your website host provider for credit
- Look at relevant keywords for your business and make a list of those you want to experiment with now.
- Start your first ad campaign and watch for action and results. Adjust as needed.

Apps

We now live in a world of "apps". Actually, most of the programs running on our computers for years now are just large applications or apps. The sudden popularity of all these little apps that can do miraculous things for us is fun and exciting. Do not be afraid of trying out apps. They can add a lot of value to your business, even replacing the tasks of an employee at times.

Recently, I installed an app called **Kit** on one of my websites. It is very useful and helpful, almost like having an assistant. Kit begins at $10 per month.

Here is what Kit can do: Each time I enter a new product, Kit will send me a text and ask me if I would like to do the following:

Run Ad (on SNS)

Update Fans (on SNS)

Both

I usually select 2 – Update Fans because I prefer to handcraft my ads for maximum potential. Instantly, Kit posts to my business Facebook and Twitter pages and does so in a beautiful way. I can adjust the app so that it only texts me when I want or not at all. I have suggested that the developers create a way to make Kit take a nap and stop sending texts. You can "wake" Kit up by just texting "Hi Kit" and the process begins.

Kit can also send emails to your customers for you if you desire. These emails can be of a thank you nature or announcing something new. The developers of this APP are creating more value and features as time goes on.

Kit works with your business Facebook and Twitter feeds currently. This saves me from having to make the posts manually and it works each day for only $10.00 per month. They have also just announced a premium version with more capabilities for $25.00 per month. Kit only works with some website platforms currently. Shopify is one of them.

https://kitcrm.com

Kit also has the ability to do some retarget marketing for you. For each person that clicked on a Facebook ad you ran, Kit can send a retarget to them showing the product again. I always love free apps, but I have to say that Kit is worth $10.00 per month.

Hootsuite is another app I am currently using. It has more features that allow you to post under different company names and with many different accounts, all for only $14.95 per month.

With this tool, I am able to log on via my computer or smart phone and schedule posts to Facebook, Instagram and Twitter. If you have more than one website, this really comes in handy. Further, it shows you how many times you are being mentioned and by whom with the date. It will show "retweets" from your Twitter account as well. What to do with this info? Try sending a promo code to those that retweet or repost your entries to get them to purchase.

Hootsuite on your desktop has a lot of options for viewing what activity is happening on all the social networking sites you have linked to it. It is constantly keeping track of this for you.

If you are a one to two person operation, you can take an hour on the weekend and set Hootsuite up to post for you throughout the week or month, scheduling those photos and posts in advance. By adding the app to your smart phone, you can then also send out more tweets and posts to Facebook and Instagram. If you only want to post to one or more social networking sites, it is just simple clicks that control that. Hootsuite includes easy to use tutorials so you can be up and running with this quickly. A full display of analytics of the action happening on each social site is included. I definitely like this app!

Other similar apps for social network updating that you may want to try include: Buffer, Sprout and Tweetdeck.

Product Reviews

There are many different apps on the market for product reviews. You will find a few that are free. Most are a very low cost. I highly recommend that you have product reviews on your site. Many consumers definitely want to read them prior to purchase. It can be difficult to get your customers to leave reviews. Brainstorm an incentive for them to do so. Remember also that the more videos you have on each product will also help to spur on sales.

Loyalty Programs

I use an app called **Sweet Tooth** that is very easy to implement and is free on Shopify for the first 500 rewards members. This app also integrates with BigCommerce and Magento users. Their site says they are adding more platforms.

I can set Sweet Tooth to reward points to every customer (including past ones) for different actions. Certainly, when they purchase they earn points, but I can award them points just for registering with my site or making a referral. The possibilities are endless. This app helps to convert browsers into shoppers wanting to collect those points. https://www.sweettoothrewards.come

Wish List

There are several apps to add a customer wish list to websites and this is smart to have. While you may have a shopping cart feature that saves what they have deposited there, a wish list is very useful and they can share it with friends or family. These apps range from free to $20.00 per month with most averaging around $4.99.

Coupon Pop-Ups

It seems like just about every site is using coupon pop-ups either immediately when you enter a site, or a few seconds later. Some give immediate discount codes or free shipping offers. If you have a business where you can set up a buy 1 get 1 at 50% off, I think this really ignites shoppers. If you have something that costs you very little but adds value to any transaction, a pop up announcing: "Free Socks with Every Shirt Purchase". I also really like exit coupons which appear right when someone is about to leave your site. It's like wait, do not go, I need to give you something. There are many that offer this. I am looking at Last Minute Coupon which has a fourteen day free trial and is $5.99 per month after that. Remember, you have no long term contracts with these apps. If they are not increasing revenue, you can drop them.

Tools For Your Business

There are many online tools for assisting you in your business. In the photo editing category, these four stand out: Pixlr – Gimp – Sumopaint – Canva. I often use Canva to create a visual item for social networking and blogs.

I'm crazy about actual physical to do lists and sticky notes. I use binders quite a bit too for organizing ideas. Many people like having these ideas, reminders and information in a digital cloud stored format. Evernote is probably the leader here. You can also try Google Keep – Todoist – Wunderlist.

For accounting purposes, I use Godaddy Bookkeeping at $9.95 per month. This is a very inexpensive bookkeeper and it works well. You may also want to look at: Shoeboxed – Quicken – YNAB (you need a budget) – Wave.

Why are so many apps free? They want you to try them out. Once you have either a larger customer base or a need for more advanced features, they hope you will convert into a paying customer.

The Soft Touch

Recently, I met with a client who needs branding and social marketing created for a real estate team. She was new to navigating the world of online marketing. In her previous job, she had conducted all of her marketing either on the phone or face to face. Having many years of direct selling with products plus thirteen years in real estate myself, I understood her marketing style and knew she had hit on something.

It is important in our world of computers and smart phones where people do not interact face to face that we do something that sets us apart from our competition. Going local in your community helps a great deal to let people know about your site. You do not have to have a brick and mortar to be a valid part of your locality.

Connecting locally in a generous way in your community is a wonderful way to help others and build your brand. I recently heard of a lady who is holding an annual maternity bra donation event in her city. Maternity bras are expensive and she enlists women to donate their gently used maternity bras to those who cannot afford them. She holds an event and enlists local media coverage. She owns a site that sells items for mothers. This is a genius idea!

Allow me to share a few ideas I have implemented in the past and some to entertain for the future:

Hand written thank you notes are a wonderful touch. If you drop ship your products, this is really important! Put a coupon or certificate inside that tells your customer how many reward points they now have and/or a discount.

A hand written note thanking a past customer for a glowing review they left for the product purchased and/or service at your site

An extra gift for anyone who had to wait a few days for some delay

Local giveaways, contests or charitable events

Talk about your business on local radio stations, television or relevant internet radio podcasts.

Have inventory you need to move out and it has not sold for a long time, who could you donate to? Can you incorporate that into an event that would provide some coverage for you?

If you sell used items such as vintage record albums and games, begin a buy-back program

Be happy to handle phone calls from customers. With ecommerce, this is often as close as you can get to a face to face conversation and it builds rapport. Make sure your customer service personnel understand this. If you talk with people for just a few moments, you will be surprised what they open up and tell you!

Your Attitude of Gratitude

Each morning, I begin my day by writing. I am usually still in my pajamas, cup of java in hand, with my spiral bound notebook (I go through a lot of these) and pen. Initially, I begin writing whatever comes into my mind.

I make sure to think about what I have to be grateful for. This could be as simple as being alive, my husband, children, or the idyllic weather that day. This is part of my secret writer's journey that I have found effective for framing the rest of my day.

I often write out my thoughts to the Almighty, prayers and wishes. I give written thanks for these things as if they have already happened. When finished, I read the often scribbled lines with strong emotion and feel myself receiving what I desire.

When I was in real estate I did this practice in a little notebook. I would write out that the property at such and such address had sold. I would visualize myself at the closing table with the buyer and seller, all of us happy and me collecting a check at the end. As I would begin my real estate work each day, I would take the little notebook out and read first the ones that had already sold and come true to reinforce to myself that this works and is possible. Next, I would read the entries of the properties still waiting to sell. So many of the properties I sold were listed with other brokers prior to me for a year or more. They were not easy sales, but somehow, my little writing practice had an effect along with smart marketing and work.

No matter your personal persuasion about spirituality or religion, I invite you to try this practice for yourself. If mornings are way too hectic, make it a nightly practice. I used to have hectic mornings. In fact, I spent the majority of my life that way and I am happy to be free from it now. I have worked for myself now for over twenty years. However, I had kids to drive to school and pick up each weekday, plus a more than full-time real estate practice. So, I do understand about being busy.

For a business owner like you, first focus on what you have. That is a key to fashioning the day before you. If you have no orders that day, but you do have website visits, give thanks for that and know that people are considering your site and actually coming to it. If this happens repeatedly, be thankful for that feedback and change your approach – figure out why they are not purchasing.

If you only have one or a few orders, be thankful for them, really feel the gratitude and commit yourself to giving those customers over the top service. If you have many orders, fuel those feelings of gratitude within yourself to keep it flowing.

As you spend this time alone with yourself in the morning or evening, write down how thankful you are for those around you that support you in your endeavors and for the fact that you seek out information needed to be better at what you do and it always comes to you.

If you are in a bad way with your business, write those feelings out and ask to be guided to finding the right people, information or things to make your business into something better. Define what is "better" and write it out as if it has already happened.

When you are not experiencing success, you will either break down and quit or have a major breakthrough and turn of events as you work through it. You may begin to think that being in ecommerce is not your forte and perhaps it is not. Write your feelings and ask to be shown the answer to this question and then have a knowing that it will come to you soon.

This daily practice allows you to stay in touch with yourself on a deeper level. One of the most surprising aspects is that it seems to birth new ideas and solutions that come to you in sudden flashes. Thank goodness you have pen and paper to capture those thoughts. Keep that nearby wherever you are throughout the day because it just happens suddenly.

Craft your own way of doing this each day and when you are super busy with business, still make time for it. That is the easiest time to quit the process because you have determined that you are too busy and things are working well.

These ideas and practices are not new and I certainly did not invent them. They play off the same principles expounded in books like *Think and Grow Rich* by Napoleon Hill and Arthur R. Pell or *Write it Down, Make it Happen: Knowing What You Want And Getting It* by Henriette Anne Klauser.

By keeping motivational and education literature and resources around you for those periods when you have 15 minutes to spare, this will assist you in framing your move forward.

Cash Flow

Although I detest the word struggle, I have perfected this term at various times with cash flow. I sell primarily brand new items and many of them must be bought in quantities. There have been many times when I needed cash for other things but my money was tied up in inventory.

The more avenues you have to raise capital, the better for your business and this holds true whether you sell on your own website, eBay, Etsy or another third party site.

Some wholesale companies may extend you credit. However, that could leave you in a pickle with trying to get things sold quickly at a lower margin just to get your bill paid with your wholesaler.

I often sell pre-owned items on eBay or Etsy to raise capital along with the new items I sell. This can be one way of increasing cash flow. Unless you have significant cash set aside, keep all of your expenses as low as possible as you venture into your own site.

Run sales and email your customers letting them know you are having a monthly clearance in your online store. When you need a boost in sales, offer a special coupon with a 3-4 day window of time in which your past customers may use it at your website.

Do everything you can to keep from borrowing money if possible. There are many lenders out there for small ecommerce businesses. Take a hard look at any fees you will be charged for the loan and the terms of how it will be paid back. With so many crowd funding opportunities, this could also be an excellent way to raise capital. As you grow, always save some money back so that you create a cushion of cash flow for unforeseen inventory purchases you may want to make or new technologies to ramp up your business.

Last Thoughts

You have reached the end of this book, but not the end of help and assistance I have to offer you. If you have not visited my website for the free resources, please do that now. Ecommerce is an evolving industry and we will learn and adapt toward our success together!

Follow this formula for success:

Have a product people want. The demand drives your potential sales.

Brand your company the same across all platforms i.e., Facebook, website, Linkedin, Twitter, Youtube, etc.

Be consistent and work it like a real business each day

Analyze: what is working? What is not?

When something is not working, change your approach.

Do not give up. The turning point in your situation can often be just around the corner.

Remember the Attitude of Gratitude and the ideas on how to start your day … or end your evening.

As I finish this writing and ready it for publishing, I want you to know that I truly appreciate you purchasing this book and would love it if you took just a moment from your schedule to leave a customer review. I am hopeful that for the small price you paid, you feel that you definitely received much more back with the information provided.

Take advantage of the free resources I have for you on my website which will enable us both together to keep up with the latest technologies that assist ecommerce businesses like ours.

As you know, my philosophy is always less is more. You will not find my email in your inbox each day. Instead, a short message will be sent maybe twice per month on information I believe you will find relevant for forging ahead and building true wealth.

With best wishes for your health and wealth,

Karen Lee Fielden
AUTHOR

www.karenfielden.com

Glossary

301 Redirect or Backlinks – links from pages within your own website or incoming links established to your site from other sites. An example: If someone has recommended your product in a blog or on another site, the backlink provides the address to get to that page on your site. Backlinks have become increasingly important for search engines, such as Google, to determine the relevancy of your site.

A/B Split Testing – using two or more variables such as subject line of an email, you can run a test with the email program to determine popularity and which resulted in more opens.

Abandoned Shopping Cart – a feature offered by some ecommerce hosting companies that allows you to be notified when someone has left products in their shopping cart on your website. You can have an email system set up that sends that person a message reminding them of the cart, maybe offering a coupon or shipping incentive.

B2B – Stands for Business to Business - A feature on your website that allows other businesses to purchase from you at a lower cost like wholesale.

Content Marketing – used primarily within blogs but not limited there. This marketing is on topic and related to the interests of those who would purchase your products, but it is not about your products. It could be described as helpful, useful, relevant information that assists you in targeting and finding your customers.

Conversions – People who come to your website and actually follow through and purchase.

Engagement – measurement of people liking, commenting, sharing your post or ad on social networks

Guest Option – customer may choose to purchase as a guest without officially registering with your site and creating a password

Hashtags – these words with the # symbol in front group subjects together across a platform or the entire internet. They are important for increasing your exposure. #sales

Inventory Management – system that keeps track of products in sold and still available.

Multichannel Selling – selling on multiple sites, not just your own.

Retargeting – an application or program that sends reminders to persons who have engaged with your site or product advertisement. This can be achieved with text, photos or both.